T0273982

THE RISE OF
WASHINGTON STATE UNIVERSITY
FOOTBALL

THE ERICKSON & PRICE YEARS

BEN DONAHUE

THE
History
PRESS

Published by The History Press
Charleston, SC
www.historypress.com

Unless otherwise indicated, all images are courtesy of WSU Libraries'
MASC.

First published 2023

Manufactured in the United States

ISBN 9781467152914

Library of Congress Control Number: 2023937164

CONTENTS

PROLOGUE

At seventy-two years young, Dennis Erickson was returning to football. Well over forty seasons as a gridiron coach were in his rearview mirror when Erickson stepped away from the game after the 2016 season. The last three years of his career had been spent as the co–offensive coordinator, assistant head coach and running backs coach for the University of Utah. Then, Erickson retired to his house by the lake in Coeur d'Alene, Idaho. He didn't unplug himself from the game completely. It was quite the opposite, as a matter of fact. "I'm a couch potato on Saturdays," Erickson said in a *Salt Lake Tribune* interview in 2019. "I have three TVs and a clicker," he said. "It's fun watching my friend Kyle [Whittingham] coach at Utah and my friend Kalani [Sitake] coach at BYU. I go visit some of the places I used to coach—places like Miami and Oregon State and others. And I live my life. It's a good life."

Erickson deserved to settle down and relax. He had coached all over the country during his career, including stops in high school, college and the National Football League. Erickson had demonstrated his ability to mold football offenses into his image. What more did he possibly have to prove? In other words, why, at seventy-two, was he returning to the game?

"What else would I do?" he asked.

Erickson had been offered the opportunity to coach the new Salt Lake Stallions of the Alliance of American Football (AAF). The AAF was formed in the fall of 2018, and Erickson was consulted on the groundwork needed to get the league up and running. Bill Polian (AAF cofounder) and Steve

Spurrier, both college and NFL legends, had regular conversations with Erickson during 2018. Spurrier, who was seventy-three at the time, jumped into the league with both feet. As the head ball coach (his vernacular) for the Orlando Apollos, Spurrier would be leading his sixth organization. It didn't take much convincing, then, for Polian and Spurrier to talk Erickson into joining the AAF.

"It sounded like fun," Erickson explained to the *Tribune*. "Coaching is what I do. You can only play golf and go fishing for so long. I'm excited about it."

As the AAF began play in 2019, reports surfaced that the league was already in financial trouble. When asked his opinion on the state of the league, Erickson scoffed at the notion. "We're in good hands financially. Nobody's worried about it. The guy who came in—Tom Dundon [owner of the NHL's Carolina Hurricanes]—wanted to invest $250 million. He was already involved before this became public," Erickson said.

Unfortunately, the rumors turned out to be true. By early April 2019, Dundon had suspended operations and the AAF was shuttered. Each team had been scheduled to complete ten games during its inaugural year. Instead, only eight weeks were completed. Erickson's Stallions finished the season 3-5.

"I'm extremely disappointed," Polian told the Associated Press by phone from Charlotte, North Carolina. "On the one hand it was kind of our wildest fantasies come true. It all came true and now it's all come crashing down."

Erickson returned home to Idaho not long after the abrupt conclusion to the Stallions' season. It is unlikely he will return to coaching again. Although, you never know when Erickson might think another football idea "sounds fun" and comes back for just one more year.

It's too bad that Erickson's career had to end the way it did. His departure left a number of young players without access to his immense knowledge of football. For decades, Erickson was one of a number of bright innovators in the game. He sparked fan and alumni interest at each of his college and pro stops and mentored countless young coaches in the nuances of the game. Erickson's journey from a scrappy college quarterback to an offensive guru was forged through hard work and dedication to his craft. Along the way, he developed a special camaraderie with his coaching peers and found joy in working with the athletes who played for him.

Erickson also took delight in seeing his childhood friend Mike Price find success in the coaching world. The two had grown up together and were teammates at the same Everett, Washington high school. After graduating, Erickson and Price played college football and then worked their way through the ranks as college assistants. Eventually, both became head coaches at Washington State University (WSU). Erickson came first in 1987, and Price followed in 1989.

Without a doubt, the WSU football program grew by leaps and bounds under both coaches. During their tenures, Erickson and Price guided WSU to six bowl games combined, including two Rose Bowls. Before the two arrived, the program had been to three bowl games total. From 1945 to 1986, WSU football had thirteen winning seasons under nine head coaches. Erickson and Price had seven winning seasons between them over sixteen years. The Cougars have had talented players in the past. However, while at WSU, Erickson and Price developed several future NFL players, including two quarterbacks who would become first-round draft picks and a third signal-caller who was the second overall pick of the NFL Supplemental Draft. For a university based in a small town in eastern Washington, this is quite an accomplishment.

The program that Erickson kick-started and Price built would be the impetus for many exciting years to come. Their brand of football would establish a precedent that future WSU coaches hoped to aspire to. These are the stories of Washington State football's rise to prominence under Dennis Erickson and Mike Price.

ACKNOWLEDGEMENTS

My love for the game of football officially began on January 24, 1982. That day, the San Francisco 49ers faced the Cincinnati Bengals in Super Bowl XVI. Watching the game with family and friends, I was mesmerized by the play of Niners quarterback Joe Montana as he went toe-to-toe with Bengals signal-caller Ken Anderson. Initially, the game was a tad boring as San Francisco took a 20–0 lead into halftime. In the second half, Cincinnati made it interesting until the end, when Montana and the Niners finally pulled out a 26–21 win. After that game, I spent the next several years consuming everything about the history of football. I eventually played the game, then became a coach and later worked for two professional indoor football league franchises.

When I was in high school, I learned that Dennis Erickson, then the coach of the national champion Miami Hurricanes, had played college ball at Montana State University. Furthermore, he began his coaching career at Billings Central High School in Billings, Montana. What a small world! At the time, I was attending Billings Senior High School and would later attain two degrees from Montana State. I continued to watch Erickson's career with great interest and also kept an eye on his former program, Washington State. Under Erickson's longtime friend Mike Price, the Cougars developed great quarterbacks who were high draft picks and would occasionally appear in the Rose Bowl. I was astounded by this, because the Cougars seemed dormant for much of their existence. Suddenly, they were playing in one of the biggest games of the year.

That background paved the way for my interest in writing this book. I pitched the idea in early 2022 for a manuscript about the Washington State football program during the Erickson and Price years to Arcadia Publishing. Thankfully, Arcadia editor Laurie Krill worked with me on forming my proposal until the project was greenlit. I sincerely appreciate Laurie and the time she has spent reading through rough drafts and offering me feedback. She gave me the confidence to complete something I've wanted to do for decades. I'd also like to thank Dr. Geoffrey Gamble, who helped get the project started by making introductions between me and some of my interview subjects. A hearty thanks to Dennis Erickson, Mike Price, Timm Rosenbach and Mike Leach. Coach Leach passed away suddenly on December 12, 2022, and I count myself fortunate to have had the opportunity to share some time with him. I will be forever grateful that each of these men took time out of their busy schedules to answer my many questions and put up with my utter fascination with their careers, offensive philosophies and teams coached. Thanks as well to archivist Mark O'English and associate athletic director Bill Stevens, who provided me with the pictures in my book.

Jimmy Swartz, founder of brownsnation.com and several other websites, gave me an opportunity to be a contributing writer in 2019 after several years in sports administration and teaching. Jimmy patiently helped me rediscover my writing voice; I have been obsessively writing ever since. I doubt I would have had the courage to attempt such a feat without Jimmy's trust in me as a writer. I would like to thank my family and my parents, Tom and Louise, for always encouraging me and helping me get out of my comfort zone. Last, and certainly not least, thank you to my wife, Micki, for her patience and belief in me. I couldn't have done this without you, my dear!

1

ALL DUE RESPECT

Although this is a book dedicated to the Dennis Erickson and Mike Price years at Washington State, it would be egregious to disregard the players and coaches who came before them. A number of notable coaches and players represented the Cougars over the years and put the public spotlight on Pullman, Washington.

The football program at Washington State experienced its origins in 1894, when the school was named Washington Agricultural College (WAC). For the first two-plus decades, the team itself cycled through a number of nicknames, all reflecting the area's agricultural roots. At various times, WAC was called the Farmers, the Aggies, the Hayseeds and the Potato Diggers.

William Goodyear was the first head coach in the program's history, and he served in that capacity for only one season. Goodyear was a prominent newspaper editor and reporter for several papers in the area and also dabbled in politics. After accepting the job as WAC's football coach, Goodyear would travel from his home in Palouse, Washington, to coach his team each evening. Of course, calling the position a "job" is a stretch. Goodyear was not paid for his time and travel. Nevertheless, he taught his charges the fundamentals of the game and prepared them for the rigors of college football.

On November 18, 1894, the team traveled eight miles to Moscow, Idaho, to face the University of Idaho. In the first game in program history, WAC beat Idaho, 10–0. Unfortunately, the thrill of victory was met by the agony of defeat eleven days later.

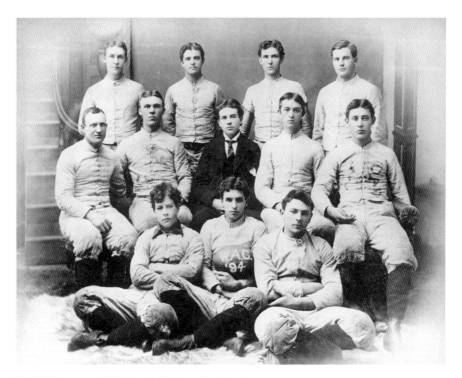

WAC's first team, 1894 (coach William Goodyear).

WAC next played the lads from Spokane High School and was soundly beaten, 18–0. Perhaps mercifully, that would be the final game the young team would play in 1894. Goodyear did not return for a second year and ended his career as a college football coach with a 1-1 record.

After a series of one-and-done coaches came and went after Goodyear, William L. Allen was hired in 1900 and became the first head coach in program history to be paid for his time. Allen would coach for two different seasons and leave with a 6-3-1 overall record.

WASHINGTON AGRICULTURAL COLLEGE BECAME Washington State College (WSC) in 1905. One year later, head coach John Bender's squad accomplished a rare feat when his team went 6-0 and defeated all of their opponents by a combined score of 44–0. In 1907, WSC had five more shutout victories and lost only once, a 5–4 setback to Idaho. WSC's football program first gained national attention in 1915, when William "Lone Star" Dietz arrived. Dietz had played football at the infamous Carlisle Indian School in Pennsylvania

Right: William "Lone Star" Dietz.

Below: "Lone Star" Dietz with his 1915 WSC team.

alongside the legendary Jim Thorpe. It was at Carlisle that Dietz first learned the game from Glenn "Pop" Warner. Warner is considered one of the forefathers of American football.

After his playing career ended, Dietz stayed on at Carlisle as an assistant coach for Warner. In 1915, Dietz headed west to Pullman to become the next head coach at WSC. Using the lessons he learned during his time with Warner, Dietz quickly whipped his new team into shape.

Right out of the gate, the team handily defeated the University of Oregon, 28–3, at Rogers Field in Pullman. In their second game of the year, WSC traveled to Oregon Agricultural College (now known as Oregon State University) and crushed the Aggies, 29–0. Next up was the "Battle of the Palouse" in Moscow, Idaho. The much-anticipated game against Idaho did not live up to the hype, and WSC left with a resounding 41–0 victory.

In games four and five, WSC hammered the University of Montana and Whitman College of Walla Walla, respectively, by a combined score of 44–7. The Gonzaga Bulldogs were the next victim, falling to WSC, 48–0, in the season's final game.

Above: WSC play versus the University of Montana, 1915.

Opposite, top: WSC runs a play during the 1915 season.

Opposite, middle: Pullman residents welcome home the WSC team after their win in the 1916 Rose Bowl.

Opposite, bottom: Pullman, Washington residents welcome home Coach Dietz after the 1916 Rose Bowl victory.

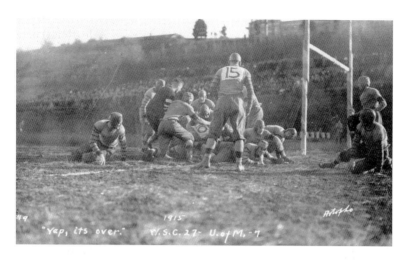

"Yep, its over." 1915 W.S.C. 27- U. of M. -7

...S. welcomes "OUR CHAMPIONS"

LONE STAR! LONE STAR! YIP. YIP. YOU! HOW WE LOVE YOU! OH. YOU SIOUX!

Coach Dietz visiting WSC in 1919.

WSC's undefeated record and lopsided wins made news nationwide and caused people to take notice of the tiny school in eastern Washington. Remarkably, the WSC football team was invited to Pasadena, California, to play in the Rose Bowl. At the time, the Rose Bowl was the only bowl game in the nation, and 1916 marked just the second-ever Rose Bowl contest. In front of approximately ten thousand people on January 1, 1916, Dietz's squad blanked quarterback Fritz Pollard (the first Black player in Rose Bowl history) and the Brown University Bears, 14–0.

WSC's 7-0 record was the most wins in program history. Furthermore, Dietz's team accumulated an astounding 204 points for the year and surrendered only 10. (In 2014, Resolution 8715 from the Washington State Senate was adopted, naming the 1915 WSC squad as national champions.) During the next two years, WSC compiled a 10-2-1 combined record, including a 6-0-1 mark in 1917. Dietz left the school with a 17-2-1 overall record after the 1917 season. He would eventually coach at several stops, including Purdue University, Louisiana Tech, University of Wyoming, Stanford University, Temple University and in the National Football League with the Boston Braves.

TWO SEASONS AFTER DIETZ's departure, during Gus Welch's first year as WSC's head coach in 1919, the program officially became the "Cougars."

According to legend, the team returned from Berkeley, California, on October 25 after playing Cal. Members of the team said that newspapers in Berkeley had written that WSC fought like cougars during their 14–0 win. Others said a cartoonist depicted the WSC team as cougars. Either way, the student body loved the idea, and the cougar became the permanent mascot of the program on October 28, 1919. Welch would post a 16-10-1 record in four years, followed by Albert Exendine's 6-13-4 record from 1923 to 1925.

In 1926, Orin Ercel "Babe" Hollingbery arrived as the Cougars' next head coach. Four years was previously the longest any coach had committed to the program. Hollingbery would break that mark and then some. For the next seventeen years, he guided WSC and established a consistent winner.

Hollingbery had grown up in the San Francisco Bay area and never attended college. He greatly enjoyed the sport of football and coached high school teams throughout the area. Hollingbery once coached three different high school teams in the same season, a feat unheard of today. He was also a renowned businessman who owned several gas stations.

The 1930 WSC team on their way to the Rose Bowl, stopping by one of coach Babe Hollingbery's gas stations.

Coach Babe Hollingbery working with players at practice.

After taking the job at WSC, Hollingbery hoped to reverse the team's recent slide of four straight losing seasons. He didn't have to worry. As soon as he stepped foot on the WSC campus, the Cougar football team appeared to transform overnight. For the next several years, the Cougars played good football. From 1926 to 1929, WSC was a combined 26-9-2, including a program-record ten wins in 1929.

In 1930, Hollingbery and the Cougars caught fire again. During their first game of the year against the College of Idaho, WSC cruised to a 47–12 win. The team faced Cal next and blanked the Golden Bears, 16–0. On October 11, the Cougars barely edged USC, 7–6. Against Gonzaga and the University of Montana in the next two weeks, WSC won by a combined score of 85–0. After a 7-point win over Oregon State on November 1, WSC went across the Idaho border into Moscow and beat the Vandals, 33–7.

The following week, the team traveled to Seattle to take on their in-state rival, the University of Washington. In a taut battle of heavyweights, the Cougars edged the Huskies, 3–0. WSC grew their national exposure by playing in Philadelphia two weeks after the Washington game and toppled

The great Mel Hein.

Villanova, 13–0. For the season, the Cougars were 9-0 and had outscored their opponents 218–32, including five shutouts.

There is no doubt that Hollingbery was a great coach. However, another reason WSC was so successful was the athletes who played for the program. On the 1930 team alone, Mel Hein, Turk Edwards and Elmer Schwartz stood out.

Hein was a six-foot, two-inch center and linebacker hailing from Burlington, Washington. He was as rough and tumble as they come and gained the nickname "Old Indestructible." After a standout career at WSC, Hein starred as a center for the New York Giants from 1931 to 1945. During his time with the Giants, Hein won two league championships and was named the NFL's Most Valuable Player in 1938. Furthermore, Hein was selected to the NFL's 1930s All-Decade Team and the 75th Anniversary and 100th Anniversary All-Time Teams. He was eventually inducted into both the Pro Football and College Football Halls of Fame.

Edwards was a no-nonsense, six-foot, two-inch, 255-pound brute at offensive tackle. He came to WSC from Clarkston, Washington, and played

Mel Hein and Miss Spokane.

with the Cougars through the 1931 season. After graduation, Edwards was pursued by no less than three NFL teams. He eventually chose the Boston Braves and played with the franchise for nine years, winning a world title in 1937. Edwards was selected as a member of the NFL's 1930s All-Decade Team and named one of the 70 Greatest Redskins. Much like Hein, Edwards was later inducted into the Pro Football and College Football Halls of Fame.

Top: Turk Edwards.

Bottom: Elmer Schwartz.

Schwartz, also known as "Elmer the Great," was the Cougars' team captain and played with the squad through the 1930 season. After leaving Pullman, he played for three NFL teams in three years.

At the conclusion of WSC's 1930 season, the Cougars found out they had one more game to play. For the second time in program history, the team was invited to play in the Rose Bowl. Unlike in 1915, the game would be played in Rose Bowl Stadium. The venue had been built in 1922 and had a seating capacity of sixty thousand.

Every seat was filled for the January 1, 1931 game against the University of Alabama. Like WSC, the Crimson Tide was undefeated and had given up just 13 points for the season. Unfortunately, the Cougars were never a threat, as Alabama's strong offense scored 3 touchdowns in the second quarter on the way to a 24–0 victory.

With the sting of the Rose Bowl loss behind him, Hollingbery coached WSC for another twelve years. Along the way, he continued to develop iconic athletes for the Cougars program. Two memorable players from that era were Ed Goddard and Bill Sewell. Goddard was a star quarterback and punter for WSC from 1934 to 1936 who was responsible for over 60 percent of the team's points during his career. Each year, the "Escondido Express" (a nickname from his high school playing days in Escondido, California) was named a first-team All-American. He was also named a consensus All-American after the 1935 and 1936 seasons. Goddard finished in the top ten of the first-ever Heisman Trophy balloting in 1935. After graduating, Goddard played two years in the NFL for the Brooklyn Dodgers and Cleveland Rams.

Sewell played quarterback for the Cougars after Goddard left and led the nation in pass completions in 1941. Additionally, he set a new record at

Left: Schwartz and Hein with Radio Pictures actress Irene Dunne at the January 1931 Rose Bowl.

Below: Irene Dunne with Alabama and WSU captains before the 1931 Rose Bowl game.

Opposite: Ed Goddard in action.

the time for total offense on his way to first-team All Coast and third-team All-American.

Coach Hollingbery left Pullman after the 1942 season with a 93-53-14 record. His win total is the most in program history. During his career, Pullman was an intimidating place for opponents to play. Hollingbery's teams from 1926 to 1935 did not lose a single home game. Hollingberry is also credited as the creator of the East-West Shrine Game, which consists of players from the eastern and western United States playing each other. The game is still played today and is known as a de facto scouting event for NFL personnel. Hollingbery was inducted into the College Football Hall of Fame in 1979.

After Hollingbery exited the program, the next several decades would not be kind to the Cougars. There were memorable moments and coaches during this period, however. In 1956, Jim Sutherland was hired and eventually implemented an early form of the run-and-shoot offense. Typically, the run-and-shoot is a pass-happy attack with four wide receivers and a lone running back. After the ball is snapped, the receivers change their routes while in motion based on what the defense does.

The offense had been around since Glenn "Tiger" Ellison first developed it in the 1930s. For the Palouse, the run-and-shoot was rather unique. Unfortunately, despite steady play from quarterbacks Bob Newman (1956–58) and Dave Mathieson (1961–63), the Cougars didn't quite have the personnel to be effective in Sutherland's offense. During his eight-year tenure (1956–63), the Cougars had just four winning seasons, although his 1958 squad did boast a top-ten ranking.

Jim Sweeney was hired by the recently renamed (in 1959) Washington State University in 1968 after leading the Bobcats of Montana State University for five seasons. While at Montana State, Sweeney won three Big Sky Conference championships and posted an overall record of 31-20. Regrettably, even with a huge upset of tenth-ranked Stanford in 1971, he did not find the same success at Washington State. During his eight years with the Cougars, Sweeney had one winning season (1972) and an overall record of 26-59-1.

However, it is not so much the win/loss record that Sweeney is remembered for. Instead, it was his influence on young coaches and recruits. During his time at Montana State, Sweeney's quarterback in 1966 and 1967 was Dennis Erickson. Erickson earned all-conference honors while playing under Sweeney's tutelage and credits Sweeney as a "huge influence in his life." While Sweeney was coaching at WSU, Erickson's father, Robert "Pinky" Erickson, served on Sweeney's staff. Dennis Erickson joined Sweeney's Fresno State University staff when the latter left WSU after the 1975 season.

Sweeney's staff is also credited with recruiting Jack Thompson out of Evergreen High School in White Center, Washington. WSU was fortunate to get Thompson, who had been a lifelong Washington Huskies fan. "My dad loved the Huskies and I idolized Sonny Sixkiller," Thompson said in 2002. "I grew up in Seattle. There was no question in my mind that I'd be a Dawg."

Quarterback Jack "Throwin' Samoan" Thompson.

As fate would have it, Thompson had a falling out with the Husky coaches during his recruitment and reversed course to Washington State. Although Sweeney coached Thompson for only one season (1975), Thompson's signing would eventually be viewed as a turning point for WSU football in the modern era. Specifically, the quarterback position for the Cougars became a perpetual training ground for aspiring professional quarterbacks.

With Sweeney's exit to Fresno State, Jackie Sherrill was hired to lead the Cougars in 1976. Sherrill arrived from the University of Pittsburgh, where he had been the Panthers' associate head coach and defensive coordinator for three seasons. Sherrill stuck around for only one season before returning to Pitt to serve as their head coach.

WSU's 3-8 record in 1976 somewhat obscured Jack Thompson's phenomenal sophomore season. That year, he completed over 58 percent of his passes for 2,762 yards, 20 touchdown passes and 14 interceptions. His play in '76 led Harry Missildine of the *Spokesman-Review* of Spokane, Washington, to dub Thompson the "Throwin' Samoan" on account of the quarterback's American Samoan heritage.

Thompson continued to lead the Cougars during Warren Powers's single season as head coach (1977). As WSU improved to 6-5 that year, Thompson again passed for over 2,000 yards, along with 13 touchdowns and 13 interceptions.

In 1978, Jim Walden became the Cougars' third head coach in as many years. Fortunately for WSU, Walden would continue in this capacity for many more seasons. The '78 team regressed to only three wins, but Thompson was a steady hand. He ended his senior campaign with 2,333 passing yards, 17 touchdowns and 20 interceptions. Accounting for 351 passing yards during his freshman season, the Throwin' Samoan's 7,818 total career yards were a three-year best in NCAA history at that point. He set conference records for total attempts (1,086), completions (601) and TD passes (53). As a Cougar, Thompson was named all-conference and All-American three times. After his final season (1978), Thompson finished ninth in the Heisman Trophy balloting.

In the 1979 NFL Draft, Thompson was selected third overall in the first round by the Cincinnati Bengals. Despite his many college accolades, Thompson did not find success in professional football. He started only five games as a Bengal in four seasons before finishing his career in Tampa Bay in 1983 and 1984.

With Thompson's departure to the NFL, Walden needed to find another signal-caller for the Cougars. He would find temporary success with Samoa

Jack Thompson and his offensive line.

Samoa in 1980 and then with Clete Casper and Ricky Turner in 1981. Overlooked on the bench during the 1981 season was Mark Rypien. Rypien, a high school All-American from Shadle Park High School in nearby Spokane, saw very little action in his first year as a Cougar. While learning the nuances of the college game, Rypien had a sideline seat for one of the best WSU football seasons in program history.

The '81 team was not predicted to do anything special that year, especially given their 4-7 finish in 1980. Surprisingly, WSU shot out of the gate and began the season with five consecutive wins. The victories included a three-point win over eighteenth-ranked Arizona State on September 26 and back-to-back shutouts of the University of Pacific and Oregon State in early October. A 17–17 tie against UCLA was followed by a rout of the University of Arizona. The program next traveled to Los Angeles for a date against USC; the Trojans won handily, 41–17. The next two games against Oregon and Cal saw the Cougars win by a combined score of 58–7. Then, in the Apple Cup against Washington to end the season, the Huskies defeated their cross-state rival, 23–10.

The Cougars' 8-2-1 record that year was good enough for an invite to the Holiday Bowl against fourteenth-ranked BYU. It was an exceptional achievement for WSU, as the Holiday Bowl was just the third postseason bowl game in program history. As the contest got underway, it looked initially like Washington State was in over its head. By halftime, BYU, led by flamboyant quarterback and future NFL star Jim McMahon, was dismantling WSU, 24–7. In the third quarter, BYU scored on an interception return to put the score at 31–7. Just when things looked hopeless, the Cougars mounted a comeback and scored 21 unanswered points to close the quarter. The fourth quarter would see both teams score a touchdown, but WSU ran out of time and lost, 38–36. Washington State would end the '81 season with an 8-3-1 record.

During WSU's spring drills in early 1982, soon-to-be sophomore quarterback Rypien injured his knee. The injury was serious enough that the coaching staff decided to redshirt him for the '82 season. After returning in 1983, Rypien appeared in only four games and passed for 384 yards and 2 interceptions. At that point, he considered transferring to a different school. Rypien's time at WSU was not turning out the way he envisioned as a hotly pursued youngster coming out of high school. After careful deliberation, Rypien returned to the Cougars in 1984 and finally became a starter.

As Washington State went 6-5 for the year, Rypien started in eleven games and passed for 1,927 yards, 14 touchdowns and 15 interceptions. He would be named a first-team All–Pac 10 member after the year. In 1985, Rypien

WSU quarterback Mark Rypien warming up.

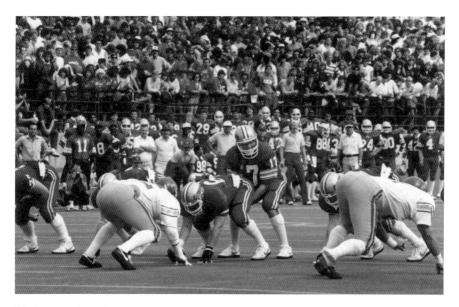

Mark Rypien in action.

continued to start and threw for a career-best 2,174 yards, 14 touchdowns and 12 interceptions. He was the "R" of the "RPM" backfield that included Kerry Porter and Rueben Mayes, a talented trio that delighted fans. Although WSU would finish a disappointing 4-7 that season, Rypien helped pull out a taut 21–20 victory over Washington in the Apple Cup.

With his collegiate career now completed, Rypien's NFL prospects looked grim. Thankfully, he was added as a late replacement player for the Senior Bowl in early 1986 and took advantage of his opportunity. Rypien's play during the game convinced the Washington Redskins to select him with the 146th pick in the sixth round of the 1986 NFL Draft. In eight seasons with Washington, Rypien started in two Super Bowls, including a win in Super Bowl XXVI. He played for six more teams before retiring from the NFL in 2002.

Jim Walden coached his ninth season at WSU in 1986 and ended the year with a 3-7-1 record. Shortly after the season ended, Walden accepted a job as head coach of the Iowa State Cyclones. Suddenly, the search was on for a new head coach for the Cougars. One of the candidates to replace Walden was Dennis Erickson. At the time, he was serving as the head coach at the University of Wyoming. After taking over the Cowboys program in 1986, Erickson led the team to six wins, a three-win improvement from 1985. Although he had just completed his first season at Wyoming, Erickson was

Left: Kerry Porter, part of the "RPM" backfield. *Right*: Rueben Mayes, part of the "RPM" backfield.

interested in the WSU job. It didn't hurt that he had ties to the program. Not only had Erickson played for former Cougars coach Jim Sweeney at Montana State, but Erickson's father had been an assistant during Sweeney's time at WSU.

In January 1987, Erickson accepted the position as the new head coach of the Cougars. For Erickson, his job was a homecoming. "It was just a matter of coming back home. We had a lot of people that were Cougars growing up, and my dad was co–head coach there for Sweeney at Washington State for three years," said Erickson in 2022. "We had a lot of connections, I guess you would say. It was an opportunity to get to Washington at that time."

By the time he arrived in Pullman, Erickson was known as an offensive innovator and turnaround specialist. His teams improved quickly at each stop in his career and were noted for their unique aerial attack. In addition to Wyoming, Erickson had been the head coach at the University of Idaho (1982–85). Both programs saw an immediate increase in wins when Erickson took over and generated excitement from fans and alumni. Erickson told the media when he arrived in Pullman that it was his goal in life to coach the Cougars.

Initially, the entire Palouse must have been concerned about this so-called offensive mastermind. In his first season at the helm, Erickson could coax just three wins out of his team. His 3-7-1 record matched exactly the record from the previous year under Walden. The Cougars' conference record of 1-5-1 was worse than in 1986.

The doubters were silent when Washington State and Erickson improved to 9-3 overall with a conference record of 5-3 in 1988. Even more special, the Cougar program returned to a bowl game for the first time in seven years. The 1988 Eagle Aloha Bowl was only the fourth postseason game in program history. The icing on the cake came when Washington State defeated a tough Houston Cougar squad (yes, two "Cougar" teams), 24–22.

That's when things really got interesting. Washington State football had experienced sporadic accomplishments for most of its existence. Erickson had come in and turned things around in two years. His success matched the turnarounds he had fostered at Idaho and Wyoming. Suddenly, Erickson was in high demand. Top college programs throughout the country wanted his services and were willing to pay for whatever he needed. Erickson assured the Pullman community that he would not leave. Then he did.

The allure of the University of Miami Hurricanes proved too much. Former 'Canes coach Jimmy Johnson was leaving to head the Dallas Cowboys. Erickson was approached about the position and was eventually convinced that the fit would be perfect. As expected, his departure was not well received by some of the Cougar faithful.

Nevertheless, Erickson was gone from Washington State and would find great success in Miami. In his stead came his longtime friend and former WSU assistant, Mike Price, who would pick up where Erickson left off. Under Price, the Cougars would ascend to heights never experienced before. In only a few short years, WSU went from perpetual underachievers to experiencing success unseen since even the Babe Hollingbery years. Without a doubt, Erickson and Price had come a long way since their childhood in western Washington.

A LIFELONG FRIENDSHIP

I f there were ever two people who were born to be football coaches, it was Dennis Erickson and Mike Price. One could say their destinies were intertwined when they found themselves running in the same circles in Everett, Washington, as kids. Erickson was born in Everett, lived for a spell in Ferndale, Washington, then returned to Everett. That's where his father, Robert "Pinky" Erickson, was named the first head football coach at Cascade High School, which opened in 1960. Price was born in Denver, Colorado, but the family relocated to Everett when Price's father, Walt Price, was named the head coach at Everett Junior College.

Back then, Everett wasn't the bustling metropolis it is today. There were two main high schools in the city at the time, Cascade and Everett High Schools, as well as a junior college. The proximity of their jobs meant that the elder Erickson and Price would frequently get together and talk shop. Needless to say, it didn't take long before their sons met each other and formed a friendship. Although they went to different junior high schools, the two hung out as much as possible. Both played youth sports but rarely faced each other, since they played in different leagues.

It wasn't until high school that the duo was able to compete together on the same team. Price was a grade ahead of Erickson at Everett High, but they both played sports for the Seagulls and thrived on the football field. What made things really interesting was the fact that Bill Dunn, the head coach at Everett High, lived next door to the Erickson family. Since the head coaches of the city's two main high schools were neighbors, things got tense at home the day before the two schools played each other. "We'd sit down to dinner the night of the game, and he wouldn't give me any information and I wouldn't give him any," Dennis Erickson said years later.

By the time Price was a senior and Erickson was a junior in 1963, they were playing on both sides of the ball. In addition to playing safety, Price was the starting quarterback for the Seagulls. Erickson also played safety but saw time as a receiver, running back and kicker. Early in the '63 season, Everett High was beaten in a close game with Seattle Prep, 14–13. The 1-point difference actually involved Erickson and Price. After scoring a late touchdown, all the Seagulls had to do was kick the extra point to tie the game. That was easier said than done. "I feel like it was yesterday that Dennis was kicking the extra points and I was holding, and I could see that my right guard got beat and the guys from Seattle Prep put one hand up and knocked it down and we lost that game," said Price in 2022.

With the difficult loss to Seattle Prep behind them, Price received more bad news weeks later. An unfortunate staph infection meant he was out of action for several weeks. The coaching staff then moved Erickson to quarterback, where he would play well and lead the team to a 9-1 record. When his infection healed, Price returned and backed up his friend. "I was out a month, and then of course, Dennis came in and did a great job and led us to all those victories. I was a backup in my senior year at the end of the year, but Dennis came in and he was better than I was anyway," Price laughed years later.

Price graduated from Everett High in 1964. Erickson played his senior year for the Seagulls, guided them to another 9-1 record and graduated in 1965. Price and Erickson would then take their athletic talents to the collegiate level, where they found different paths to success.

After leaving high school, Price spent the 1964–65 season playing at Everett Junior College. He then transferred to Washington State, where he was the third-string quarterback behind Tom Roth and Dave Peterson. The Cougars at the time were in the middle of a dry spell. Bert Clark had arrived the year before to take over for the departed Jim Sutherland and ended the season 3-6-1. Therefore, not much was expected of the team when Price arrived in 1965. But somebody forgot to tell the Cougars, and they embarked on a year to remember.

It started in the first week of the season, when WSU traveled to Iowa City to face the Iowa Hawkeyes. Neither team yielded much ground during the contest, but the Cougs finally eked out a 7–0 upset win. The following week, WSU traveled to Minneapolis to take on the Minnesota Golden Gophers.

Mike Price in action as a WSU player.

Once again, the team did just enough and defeated their favored opponent, 14–13. Two huge victories over two much bigger opponents brought attention from far and wide. Because of the close scores and nerve-racking finishes, the locals took to calling the team the "Cardiac Kids" (not to be confused with the Cleveland Browns' "Kardiac Kids" of 1979 and 1980). *Sports Illustrated* came to Pullman for a story about the surprising team from the Palouse. The excitement would only build as the 2-0 Cougs then faced their nemesis from Moscow, the University of Idaho, in their next game. For the third week in a row, the final score was close, but this time the Cardiac Kids came out on the wrong side and lost to the Vandals, 17–13.

The Cougars responded with victories over Villanova and the University of Arizona over the next two weeks. Then, on October 23, the squad was in Bloomington to face another Big Ten team, the Indiana Hoosiers. In typical fashion, WSU escaped with an 8–7 victory. One week later, the Cougs were in Corvallis, Oregon, where they dispatched the Beavers, 10–8. The University of Oregon came to Pullman on November 6, and WSU won handily, 27–7.

After an agonizing 7–6 loss to Arizona State in the season's ninth game, the Apple Cup arrived with Rose Bowl expectations. If the Cougars won the game, they would head to Pasadena for the third time in team history. If they lost, the magical season would end abruptly. There was every reason to believe that WSU would defeat their rivals, as Washington entered the contest with a 4-5 record (even though four of their losses were by four points or fewer). Sure enough, the Huskies were better than their record indicated. They ended the Cardiac Kids' season with a 27–9 victory.

Even though he was a third-string quarterback, Price also played on defense, backing up Willie Gaskins at safety. Price made the traveling team for away games and witnessed firsthand the ups and downs of the Cougars' 1965 season. In 1966, he was asked to play defense only at safety, as Gaskins had graduated. The desire to play quarterback was too strong for Price, and he transferred to the University of Puget Sound before the 1967 season. As it turned out, the coaching staff at WSU might have been accurate in their assessment of Price's quarterback skills. After starting the '67 season at quarterback for Puget Sound, Price was replaced by a freshman. "So, they [Puget Sound coaches] put me on defense anyway, but I had a nice career. I was captain and started on defense all the time so that was good, but never did make it at the quarterback position like I wanted to," Price said in 2022.

As Price was weaving a circuitous path as a college football player, Erickson accepted a scholarship to play for Jim Sweeney at Montana State University in 1965. He had gotten the attention of Sweeney with not only his play as a quarterback but also the fun fact that Erickson had defeated his father's Cascade High team twice while playing for the Seagulls. Erickson would redshirt his first year for the Bobcats and then start at quarterback beginning in 1966. The '66 MSU team under Erickson seemed to come out of nowhere and put on an offensive display. They began the season with a 4-0 record and outscored their opponents by a combined score of 170–29. At this point, Sweeney was absolutely sold on his quarterback. Already friends with Erickson's father, Pinky, Sweeney had seen Erickson play both football and basketball in high school and realized that Pinky's influence as a coach had rubbed off on his son. For Sweeney, Dennis Erickson was ahead of his time as a football player.

"(Dennis) Erickson was a coach at the age of seventeen. I always sent the plays to my quarterback, I called them myself, but when Dennis was halfway through his sophomore season, I allowed him to call his own plays," said Sweeney in *Football Revolution* by Bart Wright. "He was brilliant, but his brilliance was dedicated to football. He was smart enough that he could have done anything, but the thing that separated him was that he was such an excellent football student; Dennis was a valedictorian in football when he got here and that's what he wanted to do."

After a loss to North Dakota State in their fifth game, the 'Cats won four in a row for the second time that year. Even sweeter for MSU fans, they blanked cross-state rival University of Montana Grizzlies, 38–0. The team then traveled to Tulsa, Oklahoma, a week after the Cat/Griz game and narrowly lost to the University of Tulsa, 13–10. MSU's record was good enough to get them invited to the Camellia Bowl on December 10 against San Diego State University. The 'Cats came up short, however, 28–7.

In 1967, MSU would finish 7-3. After an 0-2 start, the team won seven in a row, including a 14–8 victory over Montana. Erickson enjoyed the

Griz win that year not only because they were the 'Cats' main rival but also because his father was part of the Montana coaching staff. Sweeney would leave the team after the season concluded to take the open head coach position at Washington State. Under new head coach Tom Parac, the 'Cats went 6-4 in 1968 and featured one of the most exciting Cat/Griz games in recent memory.

The game began with both sides engaged in a defensive battle. By the time the fourth quarter started, the Griz were leading, 10–9. Montana then scored 2 touchdowns to begin the quarter and led 24–9 with barely ten minutes to play. Just when things looked bleak, MSU running back Paul Schafer scored a short rushing touchdown with 8:15 remaining. Minutes later, Erickson found receiver Ron Bain for another touchdown to cut the Grizzlies' lead to 24–22. Miraculously, the 'Cats would take the lead when Schafer scored again with 0:12 left to cap a 234-yard rushing day. Montana almost stole the game after two plays and an unnecessary roughness penalty brought the Griz down to the MSU 13-yard line. Time expired, thankfully, giving Erickson and the 'Cats a 29–24 victory. After the game, Montana head coach Jack Swarthout gave his assessment of the outcome. "Erickson killed us," he said. With the win, Erickson, who would earn all-conference honors, owned a perfect 3-0 record against the Griz in his collegiate career and cemented his legacy as a Bobcats signal-caller.

Assistant WSU coach Mike Price, mid-1970s.

WHILE THEY WERE IN college, Erickson and Price continued to stay in touch. During the summers, they got together and caught up on their latest exploits, trading war stories about their experiences as college athletes. By the time they graduated, both men knew they wanted to continue in their fathers' footsteps as coaches. In 1969, Erickson became a graduate assistant at Montana State. At the same time, Price became a graduate assistant at Washington State. His boss? Pinky Erickson. "He [Pinky Erickson] was one of my mentors. He is the first guy who ever gave me a chance as an assistant coach," Price said in 2004.

As Price was serving a two-year apprenticeship at WSU, Erickson took a job as the twenty-three-year-old head coach at Billings Central High School in Billings, Montana, in 1970. In 1971, both men returned to their alma maters: Erickson became an assistant at Montana State, and Price became the offensive coordinator at Puget Sound. The two moved once again in 1974, when Erickson was hired as the offensive coordinator at the University of Idaho and Price found himself back in Pullman as the Cougars' running backs coach. By 1978, Price was in a completely different part of the country. He had left his home in the Pacific Northwest to work for former WSU coach Warren Powers at the University of Missouri. The following year, Erickson was hired by Jack Elway as the offensive coordinator at San Jose State. That move would prove to be a turning point in the coaching careers of both Erickson and Price.

3

FOOTBALL INNOVATION AND THE ONE-BACK OFFENSE

t can be safely stated that the need for actual strategy in the game of football began in 1905. That year, President Theodore Roosevelt threatened to get rid of the sport for good if major changes weren't instituted. Until that point, the game was little more than a group of men gaining a head of steam and slamming into another group of men. The flying wedge was a popular tactic: one team would form a triangular-shaped formation with the ball carrier as the point of the triangle. The ball carrier's teammates would form lines on either side of him and help push him forward. The result was the wedge bulldozing the opponents until the ball carrier was thrown to the ground. It didn't take long before people realized that a game in which large numbers of players were either seriously injured or died probably needed a few tweaks. In 1905 alone, nineteen football players died nationwide as a result of playing the sport. That's when President Roosevelt intervened. No less than sixty-two colleges and universities heeded Roosevelt's warning and met on December 28, 1905, to discuss rule changes. The result of this meeting was the formation of the Intercollegiate Athletic Association of the United States, which was later renamed the National Collegiate Athletic Association (NCAA).

Months later, the first legal forward pass occurred, although the use of the pass didn't gain wide use until years later. For many players and coaches, the sport was still little more than a rugby match that pitted brawn against brawn. Running plays were the primary means of getting the pigskin down the field and into the end zone. Despite the new rule changes, offensive innovation in the sport was slow to materialize. Basically, most football players and coaches at the time relied on the adage, "If it ain't broke, don't fix it." Why change something that everyone does and is, to some extent, effective?

Of course, just because something is the norm doesn't mean it should stay the norm. Somewhere along the way, a few football coaches didn't believe in the status quo and decided to start tinkering with their strategy. After all, there had to be other means of getting the ball from point A to point B besides merely taking the ball and running. For these coaches, there were specific reasons to alter what they were doing. In order to compete, they had to address their personnel or answer for necessity. Many times, both reasons required change. Two examples illustrate this point, and they both involve the early version of the spread offense and the state of Texas.

In 1927, Harvey Nual "Rusty" Russell took a job coaching at Fort Worth Masonic Home outside of Fort Worth, Texas. The Masonic Home was a place for orphaned boys and girls, which meant adolescents of all ages and sizes resided at the school. Building a football program from the ground up was no easy task for Russell. His kids were not very big, and they had no experience playing the sport. However, Russell eventually whipped his charges into shape and taught them the fundamentals of the game. It soon became clear, though, that the competition was vastly superior to his team. Russell had barely enough students to field a team, and nearly all of the kids played on both offense and defense. That meant Russell could ill afford to send his boys to slaughter. For him, it didn't make sense for his thin roster of small players to pound away against schools with big players and deep rosters. Without a doubt, his kids were tough, but sending his ball carriers into the maw of a defense already designed to prevent the run was foolish.

It was at that moment that Russell came up with an idea to spread his players a little wider than usual. To compensate, the defenders would be spread out more to cover their men, creating more openings for the Masonic boys to run through. By positioning his players farther apart on the line of scrimmage and using the running lanes (and even sprinkling in some forward passes), Russell took advantage of his players' speed. To be sure, this early form of the spread offense was still run-heavy. The primary difference was Russell's idea to use more of the field to go over and around bigger opponents. Soon enough, the Masonic Home "Mighty Mites" began defeating teams several times larger than them. In Russell's sixteen years at the school, the Mites made the state playoffs ten times. Even more astounding, the 1932 team made it to the state championship game, where they played Corsicana High School to a scoreless tie. Russell's idea led him to be called "the father of the spread," and his Mites teams would be the subject of a best-selling book that was later made into a movie.

For Rusty Russell, his need to develop a new offense was brought about by his limited personnel and the need to keep that personnel upright and (mostly) healthy. For Dutch Meyer of Texas Christian University (TCU), his desire to update his playbook came after seeing Sammy Baugh for the first time. Meyer arrived at TCU in 1923 as an assistant coach after one year in the high school ranks. After nearly a decade in that capacity, Meyer was walking down the street one day in the early 1930s and happened upon an informal, sandlot football game. One of the players had an unbelievable arm and took to slinging the pigskin around with ease. Not long after the game ended, Meyer introduced himself to the player, Sammy Baugh. It just so happened that Baugh had a scholarship opportunity with Washington State College after high school. Unfortunately, a knee injury playing baseball led to the scholarship being revoked only a month before Baugh was set to leave for Pullman. Good fortune would still favor him when Meyer told Baugh that he liked what he saw in his strong right arm and that Baugh should enroll at TCU. Baugh was sold when Meyer told him he could play other sports as well, and Baugh began attending Texas Christian.

In 1934, Meyer became the head coach of TCU and put in a new offense with Baugh as its focal point. Meyer knew a good thing when he saw it, and he wasn't about to waste the talent in Baugh's arm. So Meyer developed a different form of the spread offense (later called the "Meyer Spread"), in which he put the ends and wingbacks wider than normal. In modern parlance, think of the ends as tackles or tight ends and the wingbacks as glorified running backs/slot receivers. Meyer also had the wingback stand one step back and to the outside hip of the farthest end on the line of scrimmage. Just like the Mighty Mites, the Horned Frogs still ran the ball, but Baugh allowed them to keep defenses honest with the pass. From 1934 to 1936, Baugh, who would soon become "Slingin'" Sammy Baugh (so named after a sportswriter saw him throw a baseball), threw an astounding 587 total passes. Meanwhile, TCU accumulated a 29-7-2 overall record with victories in the Sugar and Cotton Bowls. Baugh was named an All-American in 1935 and 1936 and finished fourth in Heisman Trophy voting in 1936. He was drafted by the Washington Redskins of the NFL and played sixteen years in the league. For his part, Baugh credited Meyer with his ability to thrive as a passer and a football player.

"All the coaches I had in the pros, I didn't learn a damn thing from any of 'em compared with what Dutch Meyer taught me. Everybody loved to throw the long pass. But the point Dutch Meyer made was, 'Look at what the short pass can do for you.' You could throw it for seven yards on first down, then run a play or two for a first down, do it all over again and control the ball. That way you could beat a better team," Baugh said.

To be sure, Russell and Meyer weren't the only innovators of offensive football at the time. Nevertheless, their contributions to the origins of a more wide-open attack are well documented. In his thoroughly researched book *Football Revolution*, author Bart Wright details the formation of the spread offense and how it transformed football, particularly college football. In the early chapters of his book, Wright further explains Meyer's need to develop a new offense. Wright is also careful to point out that the Meyer Spread is not anything like the modern-day version of the spread offense. In particular, the essence of the term *spread* is slightly different in philosophy. "To Dutch Meyer in the 1930s, the concept he called the Meyer Spread meant two slotbacks lined up on the outside hip of the tackle at either end of the line of scrimmage. By the time Vince Dooley [former Georgia coach] and other college coaches heard about spread offense fifty years later the term was used more literally, with up to five intended receivers, backs, tight ends, and wide receivers stretched out across the field, literally forcing defenses to spread out."

The early use of strategic football began primarily with single-wing and double-wing formations. These were run-heavy formations that relied on precise blocking and pulling by the offensive line and deceptive ball movement by the backfield. Meyer's spread sprang out of the double-wing offense. The single- and double-wing formations begat the T formations, which included the wing T and the split T. The formation was called a "T" because, when all of the players lined up, their formation resembled a giant *T* with a single wingback. Out of these formations came more run offenses, such as the wildcat, the wishbone and the option. The wishbone has as its centerpiece the "veer," which is generally regarded as the "triple option." The option itself can be run out of the I formation, which, much like the T formation, resembles a giant *I*. Although these are just random words to those not well versed in football history, just know this: Each formation primarily involves the run game, and each uses blocking schemes designed to spring the ball carrier for big chunks of yardage. Furthermore, when the word *option* is used, it simply means the quarterback (or initial ball carrier) has options to choose from for where the ball goes. He can keep the ball or hand it off to a teammate. Each formation also involves "reading" key defensive personnel to decide where the ball needs to go and who will run with it.

From these run-based offenses came the coaches who wanted to throw the ball more often. Sure, they knew a run game was important, but they wanted more flavor in their play calling. For these coaches, it wasn't so much a lack of personnel or safety concerns that made them want to try something new. They simply wanted something different.

Russell and Meyer helped begin the forward pass trend, but the passing game would become only more complex. Decades after the early spread offenses, former college coach and NFL coach Don Coryell broke out his "Air Coryell" passing offense. The Coryell system led to the intricate West Coast offense developed by the likes of former San Francisco 49ers head coach Bill Walsh. Walsh's system begat the modern spread offense as well as the run-and-shoot offense. The modern spread has its origins with, among others, Coach Darrel "Mouse" Davis, who borrowed run-and-shoot concepts from "Tiger" Ellison. These offenses require smart quarterbacks who can decipher defenses on the fly and get the ball to as many as five different receivers. What makes these formations really exciting are the run variations that can be deployed. By using formations that simulate a pass, coaches can call a run when least expected and catch the defense by surprise.

With all these pass-happy offenses, defensive coordinators had to work overtime. That meant the development of ideas intended to at least slow down a pass-centric offense. Such defenses have included the cover two, the zone blitz, former Chicago Bears defensive coordinator Buddy Ryan's "46" defense, the double-A gap blitz and formations such as Joe Lee Dunn's 3-3-5 or former TCU coach Gary Patterson's 4-2-5. For the uninitiated, those numerals represent the number of defensive linemen first (3 or 4), linebackers second (3 or 2) and then the number of defensive backs (5 in both coaches' formations). These defenses didn't always stop the high-powered passing game, but they could slow things down if run correctly.

In the middle of all of this innovation came Dennis Erickson and Jack Elway. Elway had just been hired by San Jose State in 1979 after three years at Cal State Northridge. Although this was Erickson's first time working with Elway, the two were already familiar with each other. Like Erickson, Elway had his football roots in Washington. He had learned the game under Jack Swarthout at Hoquiam High School in Hoquiam, Washington. Swarthout was an innovator of offensive football since taking the Hoquiam job after World War II. The out-of-the-box concepts he had rattling in his head came to life when Elway joined the team as a sophomore. Elway ran Swarthout's modified T formation offense to perfection. Just as Sweeney praised Erickson's football intelligence years later, Swarthout noted that Elway was a kid ahead of his time. Elway picked up football concepts quickly and put them to use on the first try.

After graduating high school, Elway tried to play quarterback at Washington State College but was felled by a nagging injury and had to quit the team. He then played flag football with a fraternity league and served as a player/coach. It was during these moments that he would draw up exotic formations and, while playing quarterback, stand a few feet from the center before the ball was snapped. That formation is now known as the shotgun. After graduating, Elway dove right in and coached at the high school level, then community college, then at the University of Montana. Swarthout had become the coach at Montana in 1967 and hired his former quarterback. Pinky Erickson was also hired by Swarthout, and both Erickson and Elway had the good fortune of playing against Dennis Erickson's Montana State teams a few times.

In 1968, Sweeney left to become the head coach at Washington State and eventually hired Elway and Pinky Erickson as offensive coaches. By the time Elway was named San Jose State's coach in 1979, Dennis Erickson had wrapped up a three-year stint as the offensive coordinator at Fresno State. Two of those years were spent with Sweeney, who had left WSU for Fresno State in 1976. Already familiar with the Erickson family as well as Dennis Erickson's stellar football acumen, Elway hired Erickson as his offensive coordinator. With his staff now assembled, Elway got together with Erickson and his other assistants and began implementing an offense that would soon take college football by storm.

JUST A FEW HOURS down the highway from San Jose State was Jack Neumeier. Neumeier was the head coach at Granada Hills High School, located in the suburbs of Los Angeles. After a decade at the school, Neumeier's program was flatlining, and the coach needed a jolt. He was aware of what Mouse Davis was doing up in Oregon at Portland State. Davis was running a pass-happy offense with run-and-shoot tendencies. But Neumeier wasn't really enamored of the run-and-shoot. His vision of the perfect offense meant more passing but with the ability to run by pulling the linebackers away from the middle of the field.

It all came together for Neumeier one day when he watched a Granada Hills basketball game. The Highlanders were facing a big, tough, imposing team, and the ability to move the ball offensively was a challenge. While sitting in the stands, Neumeier watched as the Highlanders' tallest player (who at six feet, one inch tall served as the center for the team) was being guarded by a much taller player. The Granada Hills player would hold his hands up to serve as a target for his teammates to pass him the ball. The passing teammate could get the ball to the center, but after that, the center had to figure out what to do with the ball. It suddenly struck Neumeier that the Granada Hills basketball team was like his football team. Both programs faced opponents who were bigger than them. From his spot in the bleachers, Neumeier watched the action and realized that a player could get open for a pass not just with size and speed but with spacing and timing as well.

"I was watching this the whole time and it finally hit me," said Neumeier in *Football Revolution*. "It wasn't that hard to get the ball into the post. I'm watching basketball, and my focus was on how difficult it was for the kid to do anything after he got the ball, he was completely mismatched. I was thinking, 'This is like us in football, overmatched,' when the whole thing made sense all of a sudden. I thought, 'Wait a minute, we don't play basketball, all we're trying to do is get a few yards.' I realized if I can get a guy in front of a guy, like that center did down there, and get the ball to him in a hurry for five yards, we win that play."

Neumeier raced home after the basketball game and started taking notes. Drawing up formations in his notebook, Neumeier eventually came up with his new idea. As detailed in *Football Revolution*, Neumeier started by taking two receivers and lining them up just inside the sidelines on either side of the field. The tight end would be stationed close to a tackle on either side of the line. Then he moved the tight end halfway between a tackle and a receiver. The quarterback and two running backs were still in the backfield, but one of the backs could go in motion to either side of the field. That meant a member of the defense, either a safety or a linebacker, had to follow the man in motion. Just like that, there were four receivers and only one pass rusher to worry about. The one remaining back could either stay in to block the pass rusher or receive a pass himself. Neumeier's idea was to get the ball out quickly to a receiver, thereby neutralizing any pass rush. What was great about this design was that all these receivers and people in motion pulled the defensive coverage to those eligible pass catchers, thereby creating more space. The defense was spread thin, and because of all the receivers, each defensive back had to cover their man one-on-one. The quarterback and receivers would then work together. If the cornerbacks (who cover the receivers) hung back and gave their man some room in front of them, the quarterback would throw a short pass. If the corners lined up in the face of their man, the quarterback would throw behind the corners.

Neumeier worked on his formations a little more and fine-tuned them by designing plays out of the unique formation. He then taught his new system to his team, including his quarterback, Dana Potter. After Neumeier explained his vision to Potter, the quarterback initially thought his coach was nuts. "He might as well have said, 'We're going to all get together and flap our arms and see if we can fly,'" said Potter in *Football Revolution*. "I mean, it sounded crazy to me."

It didn't take long before Potter and his teammates picked up Neumeier's new offense and ran it to perfection. In one season, Potter went from passing for 998 total yards as a junior to 3,100 yards in his senior year. Better yet, Granada Hills came out of nowhere and won the City Section 4-A championship game. Potter went from obscure high school quarterback to prized recruit for the University of Nebraska. "I wouldn't have been recruited anywhere, had it not been for the spread," said Potter. "When you throw for more than 3,000 yards, it attracts attention."

When Jack Elway arrived at Cal State Northridge in 1976, he enrolled his young son, John, at Granada Hills High School. John Elway had been a linebacker as a middle schooler in Pullman, but his father saw his son's ability to pass and convinced him to try the quarterback position when they moved to California. As Jack Elway was building the Northridge program, his son was learning a wild new offense with Neumeier as his coach at Granada Hills. John Elway turned out to be a perfect fit as a quarterback in Neumeier's system. "When we lined up at Granada Hills, it was just a lot of fun to play and I just thought everyone had an offense like ours; it didn't sink in at first that none of our opponents were playing like us," said John Elway in *Football Revolution*.

Before long, Jack Elway took an interest in what Neumeier was doing and began bending the coach's ear during impromptu conversations. The elder Elway was so intrigued with Neumeier's offense that he implemented it himself at Northridge. In three years at Northridge, Elway's teams went a combined 20-11, including a program-record eight wins in 1976. Then, in 1979, he relocated to San Jose State, hired Dennis Erickson as his offensive coordinator and began showing his staff what Elway called his "one-back" offense. Elway also brought Neumeier to campus to show his coaching staff how to run the one-back. At first, Erickson was skeptical. But the more Neumeier explained the idea of the offense, Erickson was dumbfounded at the simplicity and effectiveness of the concepts. "He [Dennis] questioned it at first, but once we talked, he took to it immediately, " Neumeier said in 1995. "After a few minutes of general discussion, Dennis saw everything. He started drawing up plays himself like he'd known it all along."

Elway's coaching staff found that the concepts of this modern spread offense could be taught to players quickly. Oftentimes, most players had a handle on the system in just a handful of practices. Erickson enjoyed learning the offense and liked how it created mismatches against the defenses of the time. The inordinate number of receivers and men in motion pulled coverage away from the middle of the field. The one-back could hang around to block or go out for a pass himself. Part of the genius of the offense was that the linebackers, particularly the middle linebacker, had to account for a receiver. Since the middle linebacker was more equipped to handle the run instead of playing pass defense, that left the defense as a whole at a disadvantage. If defensive coordinators pulled the middle linebacker and added a defensive back to compensate for the extra receivers, the offense would then call a running play to exploit the missing linebacker in the middle of the field. Simple chess moves.

The one-back was far from some type of gimmick offense, and the nation found this out firsthand in 1980. On their way to a 7-4 record that year, which included a 31–26 victory over Washington State, the Spartans played at tenth-ranked Baylor in early November. San Jose State was a nearly 30-point underdog against a Bears team that featured Mike Singletary as its middle linebacker. Singletary would eventually become an All-Pro linebacker with the Chicago Bears and win a Super Bowl with the team. After a slow start, the Spartans were down, 15–0, in the second quarter. Then, slowly but surely, San Jose State clawed back and eventually prevailed, 30–22. During the contest, Erickson deliberately ran Singletary ragged with a mixture of pass and run plays. Singletary still had a good game, but by the end of the contest, he was gassed. "We spread them [Baylor] out. We had to get Singletary to come out of the box and play in space," said Erickson in 2022. "We weren't going to sit around and try to run the ball at him."

San Jose State's victory made national headlines that day and put Erickson in the spotlight. He had turned the tables on Singletary and his crew and defeated a top-ten team with a newfangled offense.

Singletary himself was flummoxed by the offense and shared his thoughts about the game years later. "What I remember was how different it was playing against that," Singletary said. "We did not overlook those guys, we practiced for it, we got off to a good start, it was just so different to play against that kind of football."

The offense that was designed by Neumeier and shaped by Elway was becoming an art form with Erickson. His willingness to throw convention to the wind and dive into the deep end of football innovation was revealed that day in Texas. "San Jose State built a reputation as a passing school, a giant-killer type of thing," said then Spartans quarterback Steve Clarkson, "and it all started in that game. Not taking anything away from Jack, because I love Jack, but that was all about Dennis, at least the offense."

With the success of the 1980 season behind him, Erickson was a finalist for some open head coaching positions throughout the country. One of the positions was at Weber State in Ogden, Utah. Ultimately, Erickson didn't get it. The other finalist that Weber State did hire was none other than Mike Price. So Erickson would spend one more year at San Jose State, in 1981. That season, the Spartans went 9-3 and finished in the top ten in the country in passing and scoring. The team also finished second in the nation with 14.2 yards per catch. Before the season began, the San Jose State staff taught their new version of the spread offense to various coaches from around the country. These men had heard about the upset the Spartans pulled against Baylor and wanted to see what all the fuss was about. One of the visiting coaches was Price. Having been in regular touch with his friend through the years, Price viewed the visit as an opportunity to catch up with his pal as well as learn about the one-back offense. Erickson gladly showed Price and his staff the nuances of the game, and the Weber State staff returned to Utah. While Price was installing and running the one-back in Ogden, Erickson coached the '81 season at San Jose State. When the season concluded, even more colleges sought the services of Erickson, and he accepted an offer from the University of Idaho to be their new head coach.

4

THE ONE-BACK GAINS ATTENTION

Mike Price returned to Utah with giddy anticipation of what the one-back could do for his program at Weber State. The football program had been through eight straight losing seasons before Price arrived. In fact, the last winning record for the school was in 1971. Price was determined to shake things up with this new offense and began recruiting heavily in Utah and California. He was looking for players who could adapt and who weren't afraid to step out of their comfort zone. Price found what he needed that year from quarterback Milt Myers, running back Kelvin Matthews and receivers Eric Allen, Curt Miller and Phil Swan.

After a few months of installing the one-back, the Wildcats began the 1981 season with four victories in the first five games. A two-game losing streak to Nevada and Boise State was followed by a three-game win streak, then a three-overtime loss to Idaho State to close the season. Weber State's 7-4 record was a major improvement over the previous year's 4-7 record.

"It was such a fun offense throwing the ball all over the place, winning, it didn't take long and everybody loved it," said Price in 2022.

It wasn't just the offense that was clicking on all cylinders; the defense had some teeth as well. Price had surrounded himself with young, talented coaches who would find success on their own years later. The defensive coaching staff alone boasted the likes of Dave Campo and Mike Zimmer, who both became head coaches in the NFL with the Dallas Cowboys and Minnesota Vikings, respectively.

The year 1982 marked the first season of Dennis Erickson's tenure as head coach with the University of Idaho Vandals. He already had ties to the community from his two years as offensive coordinator for the school in 1974 and 1975. This time around, Erickson brought the one-back offense with him and began recruiting heavily from the junior colleges in California, where he already had connections. "I was the first one to bring the offense to the Big Sky Conference, and then Dennis was the second one to bring the offense to the Big Sky. So it was pretty cool," Price reminisced years later.

Erickson himself had a talented staff that included his father, Pinky, as the tight ends coach. Other coaches included John L. Smith, Chris Tormey and Keith Gilbertson. Smith eventually became a head coach at various college football factories such as Louisville, Michigan State and Arkansas. Gilbertson spent most of his career in the college ranks, interspersed with two stints with the Seattle Seahawks. Tormey was a respected college coach who also found employment in the Canadian Football League.

The '82 season didn't start off as Erickson would have liked. Although his charges were prepared, the Vandals lost the Battle of the Palouse to Washington State, 34–14. Two victories later, the 2-1 Vandals, led by quarterback Ken Hobart, faced off against Mike Price and Weber State (who were in the middle of a 4-7 season). The two longtime friends and their similar offenses went toe-to-toe before Idaho eventually prevailed, 35–34. One week later, Erickson's team made national headlines when they defeated Iowa State, 38–13. It was an embarrassment for an I-AA program like the Vandals to come into Cedar Falls, Iowa, and blow out a I-A school. The victory once again placed Erickson's name at the forefront of the national conversation regarding an odd offense that was shocking bigger opponents.

A loss to the University of Montana preceded four straight wins and then a loss to end the season to the University of Nevada. Idaho's 8-3 record was good enough to make the I-AA playoffs, which marked the first time in school history that the football program went to the postseason. In the first round, the Vandals got revenge against the Montana Grizzlies with a 21–7 win. The Vandals were bounced from the playoffs in the second round by Eastern Kentucky, 38–30.

In 1983, Hobart and receiver Brian Allen were named to the Big Sky all-conference team. By the time Erickson and Price squared off again in mid-October, the Vandals were 4-1. This time, it was Erickson who ended up on the losing side against his friend, as the Wildcats won decisively, 28–10. Idaho rebounded from that loss to win four of their last five and finish 8-3. Meanwhile, Price's squad also improved, with a 6-5 overall record.

Erickson's 1984 team included four players who would eventually find employment in the NFL. Tom Cable was a junior guard for the Vandals and became the head coach of the Oakland Raiders in 2009. Mark Schlereth arrived as a relatively unknown recruit from Anchorage, Alaska. "He wasn't recruited by anybody," Erickson recalled in 2022. "He was a defensive lineman for a couple years and then he hurt his knee and we moved him to offense, which was the best thing that ever happened to him."

The move did prove fortuitous, as Schlereth became one of the best offensive linemen in college football. He was drafted in 1989 by the Washington Redskins and won three Super Bowls as a member of the Redskins and, later, the Denver Broncos. Scott Linehan was the sophomore quarterback for Idaho and eventually became the head coach of the St. Louis Rams. Receiver Eric Yarber, who happened upon Erickson by chance when the coach was at Yarber's junior college on a recruiting trip, signed with Idaho and was named to the Big Sky all-conference team in 1984. He was sold on Erickson's offense during his first conversation with the coach.

"He told me, 'Scouts will come to Illinois and Purdue [two schools that were recruiting Yarber], but they won't be coming to see the guy who caught twenty-five passes, they'll be coming to see the other guys, but who knows? Maybe you'll get their attention.' He said, 'If you come to Idaho, NFL scouts will come to see you, they'll have to see you because of the numbers you'll put up,'" said Yarber.

Yarber did catch a lot of passes (75 in 1985 alone), was drafted by the Redskins and won a Super Bowl with the franchise. Despite the loaded team, in 1984, Idaho had its worst record during Erickson's time with the school. That season's 6-5 mark included a second straight loss to Price's Weber State team, 40–37. Weber State would end the year 5-6.

In 1985, Linehan and Yarber got Idaho back on track. The year started off with a loss to I-A opponent Oregon State before the Vandals won six straight. Idaho's fifth win that season came at the expense of Price and the Wildcats in a thrilling 31–28 victory. Erickson's win evened the head-to-head matchups between the two. Idaho State tripped up the Vandals two weeks later, but Idaho responded with three straight wins to end the season. For the second time in four years, Erickson's team won nine games, which (along with the 1982 season) was the most wins in school history. Idaho returned to the I-AA playoffs but lost to Eastern Washington in the first round, 42–38.

In only four short seasons, Erickson's offense had helped turn around a moribund Idaho program. He had a winning record each year, which was unusual for a school that had four winning seasons in four decades.

Erickson's overall record was 32-15, which was tops in program history. His success could not be ignored, and larger schools came knocking on his door. The folks at the University of Wyoming were looking for a new head coach, and both Erickson and Price threw their hats in the ring. This time, it was Erickson who got the job over his friend.

THE 1950s AND 1960s was a good time to be a Cowboy. Specifically, the University of Wyoming Cowboys were coached well during that period. Along with several years of winning records, Wyoming also appeared in five bowl games between 1950 and 1967. They won four out of five of the contests, with the only defeat coming at the hands of the LSU Tigers in the 1968 Sugar Bowl. Then, in 1976, coach Fred Akers led the Cowboys to the 1976 Fiesta Bowl against Oklahoma, where they were defeated, 41–7. Before Erickson arrived, the Cowboys had only three winning seasons since 1976. In 1985, Wyoming was 3-8, and head coach Al Kincaid was fired by the school.

Looking over the landscape of his new program, Erickson had to dismantle Kincaid's wishbone offense and install the one-back, which was soon dubbed the "Air Express." The moniker was a little fancier than the "one-back," but it was essentially the same offense Erickson had run at Idaho. While preparing for the upcoming 1986 season, Erickson used the same formula he did after arriving at Idaho, adding receivers to play with the personnel the team already had.

The first opponent for Wyoming that season was none other than Baylor University, the school that first put Erickson's name in the national conversation when he was at San Jose State. This time, the Bears outlasted the Air Express and won, 31–28. That loss was followed by three consecutive victories including another eye-opener on September 27. The Cowboys traveled to Camp Randall Stadium on the campus of the University of Wisconsin that afternoon and dismantled their Big Ten opponent, 21–12. Little did he know at the time, but the win prompted the administration at Wisconsin to strongly consider Erickson to replace their coach, Jim Hilles, at the end of the season. (The job was later offered to Erickson, but he turned it down.)

Six games into the season, Wyoming was sitting at 4-2. Unfortunately, the Cowboys won only two more games the rest of the year to finish 6-6. Despite the disappointing end of the season, Erickson's squad won three more games than the previous year. For the Wyoming faithful, there was no reason to expect anything less than winning football in 1987.

As ERICKSON WAS SUCCEEDING at Idaho and Wyoming, Mike Price was on a perpetual seesaw at Weber State. His first year with the Wildcats in 1981 produced a 7-4 record and gave the program its first winning season in a decade. Then, between 1982 and 1986, Weber State finished 4-7, 6-5, 5-6, 6-5 and 3-8. The lack of a consistent winning record could have discouraged Price, but he kept soldiering on.

In 1987, everything finally came together for the Wildcats. Price's offense was a well-oiled machine with quarterback Jeff Carlson and running back Fine Unga, and it put up a ton of points. This included 40 points against Western State, 36 against Southern Utah, 55 against Boise State, 35 against Montana State, 38 against Idaho and Nevada, 46 against Eastern Washington and 53 against Idaho State. Those points translated to nine victories and just two losses. Weber State's record was enough to get the program into the I-AA playoffs for the first time in school history. In the first round, the Wildcats faced Idaho again and hung 59 points on the Vandals to advance. The following week, Weber State lost to Marshall University, 51–23. Despite the loss, the Wildcats' ten-win season was by far the best in school history. Even better, Price was named the Big Sky Coach of the Year for 1987.

WHILE DENNIS ERICKSON PUT the wraps on his first season at Wyoming in 1986, Jim Walden was limping through a three-win season at Washington State. It was Walden's ninth year leading the Cougars, and he needed a change. A month after the '86 season ended, he accepted a job opportunity as the head coach at Iowa State University. The search commenced for a new head coach, and WSU reached out to Erickson. Surprisingly, Erickson expressed interest. He had turned down the Wisconsin job offer and told his Cowboys players that he was staying at Wyoming. Then, while attending a coaching conference in San Diego in early 1987, Wyoming athletic director Paul Roach was contacted by WSU athletic director Dick Young. Young asked Roach's permission to interview Erickson for the job. Not even a day later, WSU announced Erickson as their new head coach.

The backlash from the residents of Laramie and the state of Wyoming was fierce, and the Cowboys players were stunned. They had not heard from their coach and only found out the news by word of mouth. Still seething, one local reporter wrote, "The Erickson Express slipped away from Laramie like a darkened train in the night." For his part, Erickson mentioned that the news of his WSU hiring was sudden and he needed to report to Pullman

Dennis Erickson during a press conference.

right away. "I had to go up to Pullman to take the job and they wanted it done right away," said Erickson. "With recruiting and all, I just couldn't get back [to Laramie]."

Erickson wasn't the first Wyoming coach to leave after one year, but the local populace still felt betrayed. They were especially vexed by his decision to pull up stakes after only one year into a five-year contract. As Erickson was busy in Pullman, his wife, Marilyn, was back in Laramie packing up their house. Threatening phone calls and rocks thrown through their windows was a common occurrence for Marilyn Erickson. Years later, Dennis Erickson expressed remorse about how he left Wyoming.

"A guy told me, sometimes there are crosses you have to bear in life. That's one of them for me," Erickson said in 2021. "That's the last thing I wanted to do, but that's how it ended up. I know nobody was very happy, and I don't blame them. I didn't particularly care about what people in the public thought, I was more disappointed in not being able to sit down and tell the players that I was taking the job before it got out. I think about it a lot, actually. It wasn't done on purpose. It wasn't done to hurt anybody."

Despite Erickson's quick exit, Wyoming did well without him. Roach stepped into Erickson's place and kept the one-back offense intact. "He's a smart man," Erickson said of Roach in 2021. "That was a heck of a move [keeping the Air Express offense] when he became the head coach. I knew they were going to have success."

Success indeed. The Cowboys won ten games in 1987 and a program-best eleven games in 1988. Between 1987 and 1990 (Roach's final year as coach), Wyoming went to three bowl games. Although they lost all three contests, two of them were close, a 20–19 loss to the Iowa Hawkeyes in the 1987 Holiday Bowl and a 17–15 loss to Cal in the 1990 Copper Bowl. After Roach left, Joe Tiller (himself a former Montana State player and coach for MSU and Washington State) took over and also left the Air Express intact. "I had no choice; they loved what Dennis had done," Tiller said in *Blood, Sweat, and Chalk* by Tim Layden. "People have asked me for years how I learned this offense. I tell them, 'Dennis left his playbook at Wyoming.' That's absolutely the truth."

In six seasons with Wyoming, Tiller had three winning seasons and one bowl appearance. He moved on to Purdue University in 1997, where he turned the one-back into his own "basketball on grass." The offense thrived under quarterback Drew Brees from 1998 to 2000. Tiller is credited with being the first coach to bring the spread offense to the Big Ten Conference, and his teams appeared in ten bowl games during a twelve-year span.

Although Erickson would admit that his Wyoming departure wasn't his best moment, he was excited to be returning to the Palouse in 1987. He told the assembled media in Pullman during his introductory press conference that it was his lifelong goal to be the head coach at WSU. His father had coached there, as had his college coach, Jim Sweeney. Erickson knew the area well due to his six years at Idaho, which was a stone's throw from the WSU campus. The stars were aligning for Erickson and his family. Despite WSU's recent less-than-stellar football reputation and the lack of local entertainment options for recruits, Erickson believed he could be successful. With his vaunted one-back spread offense, he would bring distinction and a winning attitude to the Cougars. Erickson rolled up his sleeves and prepared for the 1987 season.

5

TIMM ROSENBACH AND THE 1988 SEASON

There's a saying in football that defense wins championships. While that is certainly true in some cases (the 2000 Baltimore Ravens, for instance), football success can more readily be attributed to a specific position. More often than not, a team's fortunes will ride or die with the quarterback. Whether he is a true field general or more of a game manager, the fate of any football team will almost certainly hinge on its signal-caller.

While the one-back offense wasn't particularly difficult to learn, the system did need a good quarterback. Particularly, the quarterback had to be a good leader with a strong arm and the ability to make split-second decisions. Dennis Erickson had such leaders at San Jose State with Steve Clarkson, at Idaho with Ken Hobart and Scott Linehan and at Wyoming with Craig Burnett. Once he got the job at WSU, Erickson took a look at the Cougars roster and recognized a familiar name.

Timm Rosenbach was the Cougars' quarterback returning for his sophomore season in 1987. He had received some playing time in 1986, which amounted to 452 passing yards, 4 touchdowns and 2 interceptions. Unlike at his previous stops, Erickson was already familiar with his new quarterback. Specifically, Erickson knew the Rosenbach family well and was present later when the family experienced a moment of terrible loss.

Timm Rosenbach was born and raised in Everett, Washington, in the 1960s. His father, Lynn, was a football, track and wrestling coach at Everett Community College (ECC) from 1964 to 1967. One of the ECC athletes Lynn Rosenbach coached was Mike Price. Because Lynn was a coach in the

Erickson (*left*) and Timm Rosenbach.

Everett area at the time, the Rosenbach family became acquainted with the Price and Erickson families. Lynn Rosenbach would eventually coach under Jack Swarthout at the University of Montana. While Lynn was an assistant for the Grizzlies, Timm was playing football at Missoula's Hellgate High School. In 1983, the Rosenbach family moved to Pullman when Lynn was hired as an associate athletic director for Washington State.

Timm Rosenbach spent his junior and senior years at Pullman High School, where he initially played halfback and then quarterback for his senior year. "I switched him to quarterback because we didn't have one," said Rosenbach's high school coach, Ray Hobbs, to the *Los Angeles Times* in 1989. "He did a super job for us. He ran a couple of quarterback sneaks for over 50 yards for touchdowns."

Rosenbach was also a very accomplished javelin thrower and was recruited by schools around the country to compete in track. He was additionally recruited by Washington State and Montana State to play quarterback. Unsatisfied with the lack of choices, Rosenbach sent out tapes of his high school football games to various colleges throughout the West. Suddenly, there was interest from the University of Washington, Arizona State and Oregon State. Rosenbach liked the idea of heading off to the sun and warm weather in Phoenix and playing for the Sun Devils. Unfortunately, his father had been diagnosed with cancer and eventually lost an arm to the disease. The desire to be close to family during such a trying time led Rosenbach to make his decision on where to play next. "I was really close to going to Arizona State," Rosenbach said in 2022. "Probably the number one thing for me not going was my dad had been battling cancer for about, oh, it hadn't been that long at that point, but he'd been diagnosed with it and had lost an arm to cancer. So that was probably the key factor in me deciding to stay in Pullman."

With his father's health in mind, Rosenbach decided to remain in Pullman and play for Jim Walden at WSU. It turns out that Rosenbach was good friends with Walden's son Murray, who was in Rosenbach's class at Pullman High School. "Coach Walden will tell you that I was the easiest recruit he ever had because I was always over there eating food out of his refrigerator," said Rosenbach in 2022.

"It's hard for me to think of Timm as just another player because my son, Murray, played on his high school team and he and Murray were best friends," Walden said in 1989. "Murray and Timm were Mr. Cools around school."

After redshirting in 1985, Rosenbach saw the field for seven games in 1986. Then, Walden left for Iowa State and Erickson came aboard. The first order of business for Erickson was dismantling Walden's veer offense and installing the spread. He then taught his new team the basics during spring drills and the weeks leading up to the 1987 season. For the Cougars, especially the offensive players, Erickson's offense promised an exciting upgrade.

"We were all super excited, because the skill guys were all like, oh man, we're all going to throw it, 70 times a game, and we were fired up about that, of course," said Rosenbach in 2022. "And so, that was exciting for us but at the same time, we were like, it [the spread] was a whole different thing. We had to figure out how to be coached a little bit differently, I think, and also be able to pick up on the concepts that were being introduced to us."

The year began very well, with Rosenbach and the offense learning the new concepts just fine. They blew out Fresno State, 41–24. The season's second week had Wyoming visiting Pullman. It didn't take a genius to figure out that the Wyoming fans were out for revenge. Only a year before, Erickson was leading their team and handing out assurances that the Cowboys program was going places. In the days leading up to the game, the contest was nicknamed "The Bitter Bowl." "The fans all over Wyoming want us to annihilate them," Burnett told the *LA Times* leading up to the game. "It seems like this is the only game they really care about."

Dennis Erickson calls a play from the sideline.

It turned out to be much ado about nothing, as the Cougars pulled away from Wyoming, 43–28, to go 2-0.

"That was a real hard one," Erickson said of facing his former team, adding that some of the UW players expressed their disappointment with him after the game. "We almost got our ass beat, to be honest with you. We were all upset with what went down."

Unfortunately, the rest of the year was not very kind to WSU. They held their own for a half at Ann Arbor, Michigan, the following week but were still blown out by the Wolverines, 44–18. Then, the team lost its next three games to Colorado, Stanford and Arizona State. Even more embarrassing, Stanford and the Sun Devils crushed the Cougars by a combined score of 82–14. After a victory against the University of Arizona for win number three, WSU lost their next three games, including the Apple Cup against Washington. The Cougars then traveled to Tokyo, Japan, to face Cal in the Coca-Cola Classic, a game that was played from 1977 to 1993. After having traveled thousands of miles to play a team WSU would normally travel a few hours by flight to play, Cal and the Cougs played to a 17–17 tie.

Rosenbach's first season running the one-back was a bit rough. He passed for 2,446 yards, 11 touchdowns and 24 interceptions. His interception mark led the Pac-10 that year. "Our first year was the first year that he played in the spread, and he struggled a little bit," Erickson recalled.

"That man has to be the most patient man I've ever been around in my life as far as the coach goes, because, I mean, I would've pulled any hair out that I had," Rosenbach said in 2022 about his performance in 1987.

Rosenbach was understandably dejected after the 1987 season. The Cougars had finished 3-7-1, the same record as in 1986. Their conference record was 1-5-1, which was worse than 1986's 2-6-1 mark. Not wanting to repeat the same mistakes the next year, Rosenbach approached Erickson and suggested he play on defense.

"I remember going in there and saying, 'Hey look, maybe I'm not a quarterback.' I told him that after that year, 'Coach, maybe I should play defense,' because at the rate I'm turning the ball over, I probably ought not to have the ball in my hands," Rosenbach recalled in 2022.

Dennis Erickson at
practice.

Erickson, however, was confident in Rosenbach's ability to play the
position and was very direct in how he would need to improve in 1988.
"Dennis said, 'No, you just need to make a decision to get better. You're a
quarterback. You just got to start acting like one,'" Rosenbach added.

With that, Rosenbach and Erickson began preparing for the 1988 season.
While the coaching staff and the WSU players were confident that the
team would get better, many people in the national media were poking
fun at Erickson's expense. His vaunted one-back spread offense had gone
9-3 in 1985 while at Idaho, 6-6 in 1986 while at Wyoming and 3-7-1 in
1987 at WSU. To the naysayers, Erickson's baby was not the spectacle it
was made out to be. To them, it seemed like the higher he rose in the level
of competition, the worse his record became. Some pundits took to calling
the spread a "fad" or "gimmick" offense that was doomed to fail. It was
almost as if there was a need to return to the status quo. The majority of the
conferences and schools throughout the country were still using run-based
offenses and sneering at the one-back.

Of course, they didn't realize that change was already coming. It had
already happened in the NBA. That league was largely putting people to

sleep by the late 1970s. It wasn't until the Los Angeles Lakers drafted Earvin "Magic" Johnson from Michigan State in 1979 that the league began to transform. Under the direction of coach Jack McKinney, who installed a fast-paced, high-tempo offense that would become known as "Showtime," the Lakers began filling arenas. The rest of the league quickly took notice. Basketball fans then and now don't want to see the same old pick-and-roll. They want to see flashy and splashy, and that's what the Lakers gave them. Erickson had a similar mindset as McKinney had developed years earlier. He wanted to open up the offense and blow the doors off opponents. If his team gave up points in the meantime, so be it. His offense literally showed opposing defenses what was coming and dared them to stop it. Losing record or not, Erickson wasn't going to change a thing in 1988.

By the summer of 1988, Lynn Rosenbach's cancer was getting worse. He wasn't letting the disease stop him, though, and continued in his duties with the WSU athletic department. In early July, Rosenbach, Erickson, WSU associate athletic director Bill Moos and Cougars athletic trainer Jim Bartko were at a fundraising golf tournament in Pasco, Washington. Rosenbach had organized the tournament as a chance for Cougar fans and boosters to meet Erickson. After the outing, the four started driving back to Pullman. Along the way, Rosenbach began coughing violently and spitting up blood. They quickly made their way to Colfax, Washington, which had the nearest hospital. Erickson sat next to Rosenbach in the WSU van that Bartko was driving and encouraged his friend to hang in there. Finally, they reached Colfax and got Rosenbach in to see the doctors. While Erickson stayed with Rosenbach in the emergency room, Moos found a phone and called Timm and his mother. When Moos approached the ER after his phone call, he saw Erickson standing outside the room. The look on the coach's face said it all. Lynn Rosenbach had passed away.

Only weeks after his father's passing, Timm Rosenbach reported for fall practice with a heavy heart. He was a young man about to embark on a new season of college football without one of his biggest supporters. "It was rough, but fortunately football practice started so close after my dad died that I was able to get my mind onto other things," said Rosenbach in 1989. "You don't ever forget about someone you've been with for twenty-one years of your life. Physically they're gone, but mentally they're always with you."

Since Lynn Rosenbach was a member of the WSU athletic staff, the football team knew him well and offered their condolences to Timm Rosenbach as fall practice opened. Addressing the team, Rosenbach was direct with how he was moving forward in 1988. "I told the guys on the team that I wasn't going to dedicate the season to him because I played for him anyway," Rosenbach added. "There was no point in dedicating it to him. That's what he would have wanted me to do."

Instead, Rosenbach focused on leading the Cougars to a winning record and a bowl game. Rattling around his head was Erickson's challenge to start acting like a quarterback. The challenge motivated Rosenbach and reminded him why he wanted to succeed as a player at WSU in the first place. "I grew up on the west side of the state watching Warren Moon and Tom Flick and Robin Earl and Spider Gaines, all these guys, these Huskies. But for some reason, I always had an affinity for the guys in Pullman. I always gravitated to wanting to know what was going on in Pullman," said Rosenbach in 2022. "I mean, it was cool. That was the place for me. It was like there was a little mystery to it."

Top: Steve Broussard.

Bottom: Mike Utley.

Erickson, Rosenbach and the Cougars were set on adding a little more mystique to the program in '88. They practiced hard during fall camp and fine-tuned the one-back spread to the personnel they had. The populace of Pullman knew WSU had a talented roster and was poised to make a run. In addition to Rosenbach, the Cougars' offense boasted running backs Steve Broussard and Rich Swinton, receiver Tim Stallworth and offensive linemen Mike Utley and Paul Wulff.

As they prepared for the first game of the season against the University of Illinois, Erickson wasn't quite sure what to expect from his team. They were traveling several states away to play against a program debuting the rocket arm of redshirt sophomore Jeff George. George was a talent the Cougars prepared for, and Erickson knew his defense had to make him uncomfortable. "Jeff George concerns me," said Erickson before the game. "He's a talent. We've got to get pressure on him early with our front four."

WSU DID THAT AND then some. Cougars defensive end Ivan Cook sacked George three times. Broussard and Swinton each rushed for over 100 yards against the Illini, and the defense took care of George on the way to a resounding 44–7 victory. It was the first road win for the Cougars in over two years. Rosenbach completed 21 of 29 passes for 288 yards and 1 touchdown pass and scored on 3 touchdown runs. The emphatic win gave the team confidence and a swagger they had not felt in years. After the game, Rosenbach let the world know the Cougars were for real while also showing his mischievous side, which was fast becoming his trademark.

"We came on a business trip," Rosenbach said. "There wasn't any screwin' around in the motel and there wasn't any screwin' around on the plane on the way here. But, believe me, on the way back there'll be some screwin' around."

A week later, WSU was on the road again, this time to face the University of Minnesota Golden Gophers. Once again, the Cougars bullied a Big Ten Conference opponent with a 41–9 spanking. The loss shocked the Gophers, as they dropped their season-opening game for the first time in twelve years. Erickson's offense rolled up over 600 yards of total offense for the second week in a row. Rosenbach completed 20 of 30 passes for a career-high 353 yards and added 3 touchdowns. Broussard rushed for over 100 yards and 2 TDs, and Stallworth snagged 9 passes for 176 yards and 1 touchdown. Without a doubt, the Cougs were rolling.

"We moved the ball real well," said Erickson after the game. "It was a pretty good day. I'm surprised, but every week I start to believe more and more that we might not be too bad. And, no, I don't sweat this much. We don't win much at Washington State, so we've got to celebrate when we can."

After the contest, Rosenbach was effusive in his praise of his offensive linemen. "Our offensive line was just devastating again," said Rosenbach. "If I had the money, I'd take 'em all out to lunch. But I guess I'll just have to hug 'em and tell 'em, 'Nice job.'"

The Cougars returned to Washington to play their first game of the year at home on Saturday, September 17. The team was 2-0 and ready to show the home crowd the offense that was the talk of the nation. Their opponent was a University of Oregon Ducks squad that was also 2-0 and ready to spoil WSU's home opener. By the conclusion of the game, the fans had that old sinking feeling in the pit of their stomach. Oregon was a disciplined team and had an offense that balanced a solid pass-and-run game. They used that to their advantage by taking WSU apart, 43–28. On the flip side, it was the Cougars who were undisciplined and out of sorts, as they racked up 9 penalties.

"Penalties just killed us," said Erickson after the game. "Stupid penalties. We played very undisciplined. Unbelievably undisciplined for us."

Rosenbach missed on only 9 passes and threw for 261 yards and 3 touchdowns. But he also threw 2 interceptions. He was also irked at the officials, especially when the zebras made a controversial fumble ruling against Cougar receiver Michael Wimberly in the third quarter. After Wimberly caught a Rosenbach pass and was tackled, the ball popped loose and an Oregon player recovered. Both Rosenbach and Wimberly argued the call, saying the ground caused the fumble. The refs didn't listen and gave the ball to the Ducks.

"He was down," Rosenbach complained after the game. "That was the worst call I've ever seen in my life. They [the officials] stand there and look at each other like, 'Who makes the call?' just like the Three Stooges. Of course, I'm biased. But we're Washington State and we're playing in Pullman, that's all you should have to say."

Still disgusted after the game, Erickson told the media what the team needed to work on in the weeks ahead. "We tackled very poorly," he admitted. "It's part our fault, but they did a good job of running. We have to make tackles. We've got a lot of work to do and we have a week off. We'll probably do some tackling."

Although the Cougars were now 2-1 and scheduled to play the University of Tennessee Volunteers on their turf, the sports world had taken notice of WSU. Despite losing to Oregon, two blowouts of Big Ten opponents opened the eyes of many doubters across the country. Even Derek Loville, the Ducks' running back who rushed for 131 yards against WSU, could see that the Cougs were a team to be reckoned with going forward. "I think they'll surprise a lot of people," he said. "I think they might surprise Tennessee because they're big and physical. And they're determined."

Without a doubt, football in the American South is a big deal. The sport has hotbeds throughout the country, but it is a way of life in the South. Tradition rules the day, and by 1988, college football teams in the South were still primarily ground-and-pound offenses. Most of Tennessee's opponents were run-based teams, although their coaching staff did their best to prepare for the spread of Washington State.

In the meantime, the Cougars were preparing to go into the lion's den. Neyland Stadium, home of the Volunteers, is one of the largest stadiums in college football. At the time, the venue had a seating capacity of 91,902 after an upgrade the year before. Any opponent visiting the site experiences shivers down their spine when the Volunteer faithful exercise their lungs. Erickson was cautiously optimistic about his team's chances on October 1. Although Tennessee was 0-4 at the time, the program had been to eight bowl games in the previous nine years. Coach Johnny Majors led the Volunteers, and one could never count them out with his steady hand at the helm.

"With all the hype and everything that's going on about them losing, I think we're going to run into a hornet's nest, myself," Erickson said before the game. "Obviously, this is a different place. Football is a religion down here."

As it turns out, Erickson didn't have much to worry about. The Cougars handed the Vols their backside, 52–24, to give Tennessee their fifth consecutive loss. Vols defensive coordinator Ken Donahue, a well-respected college football coach with numerous national title rings as a coordinator, was so humiliated by the loss that he resigned after the game and never coached again. Meanwhile, everything went well for WSU that day. Even potentially costly mistakes by the Cougars ended up going their way. At one point, Rosenbach connected with Stallworth for a pass. As he caught the ball and ran upfield, Stallworth dropped the pigskin, only for it to bounce right back into his hands. Things were clicking so well that by halftime the Cougs were already in control, to the dismay of some of the Volunteer cheerleaders.

"I can remember walking in at halftime and going into the tunnel and their cheerleaders were standing there and this one cheerleader said, "Y'all got to cut us some slack. We haven't won for four weeks in a row,'" said Rosenbach in 2022. "I just started laughing at that."

By the end of the contest, the Volunteer fans were believers in WSU's potent attack. They were now believers in what Erickson was trying to do to shake up offensive football. After all, the result spoke for itself. Before the game, Rosenbach was college football's fifth-ranked passer, and he only added to his impressive numbers at Tennessee. Just four games into the season, he had already passed for 1,194 yards and 11 touchdowns. It was lost on no one that Rosenbach had only passed for 11 touchdowns total the year before. College football pundits also couldn't ignore the fact that Erickson's offense was balanced. Broussard was the nation's fourth-ranked running back before the Tennessee game and then added 133 yards against the Vols. Additionally, Broussard was a lethal receiver out of the backfield. At that point, the man teammates called "Bruiser" was starting to creep into the Heisman conversation, though voters wanted to see what he could do against better-ranked opponents. Regardless, as the Cougs headed for home, they couldn't help but feel good about where they were.

"We were just rolling during that Tennessee game," said Rosenbach in 2022. "When we won that game, we were pretty confident in ourselves."

Present that day was Tennessee defensive backs coach Kevin Steele, who would replace Donahue after the game. The defensive staff had prepared as best they could before meeting WSU. But when the game concluded, Steele realized that the college game had changed forever. Because of the spread offense, the college programs in the South were put on notice.

"We all had trouble that day against Washington State," said Steele. "It's hard to put it out of your mind. As far as I know, that was the first time a team from out West came into the South and really just put on a clinic on where football was headed. That's when I would say college football started changing because of the spread, 1988, or the late '80s in general."

A year after playing Cal to a tie in Japan, the Bears were in Pullman to try and disappoint the home crowd for the second time that season. To make matters even more tense, the contest was eighteenth-ranked WSU's homecoming. The year before, a large swath of fans left the homecoming game early as the Cougs were getting blown out by Stanford. There was a strong hankering to give the Wazzu fans a treat and take Cal down a peg or two. "This is homecoming, and a lot of us want to make up for what happened last year against Stanford," said Erickson before the game. "There's a lot of incentive."

Cal entered the game with an identical 3-1 record as the Cougs and was gunning for their first 4-1 start since 1978. They had a talented defensive front that promised to challenge Rosenbach, who entered the game as the nation's second-leading passer. Instead, Rosenbach and the Cougars dismantled the Golden Bears, 44–13, to win their fourth game of the year and keep the homecoming crowd in their seats for the entire afternoon.

As the calendar turned to mid-October, the Cougars looked to continue their winning ways against their next two foes, the University of Arizona and Arizona State. They proceeded to drop two in a row, a 45–28 loss to the Wildcats and then a close 31–28 loss to the Sun Devils. Rosenbach and the Cougars were driving late in the game against ASU for the go-ahead score, only for the quarterback to throw a pick in the end zone. Despite the setbacks, the team was not going to give up on the season. They knew they were better than their 4-3 record indicated and were determined to turn things around.

"I just remember after that game just how we all rallied together and just said, 'That's it, that game shouldn't even been close. We shouldn't have been in that as we just got a big challenge coming up and we're going to go beat these guys and we're not going to lose another game.' I mean, that was the feeling in our locker room at that time," said Rosenbach in 2022.

IF THERE WAS A game in the 1988 season when the Cougars needed to show they were a legitimate program, it was the contest on October 29, 1988. That day, WSU traveled to Pasadena, California, to face the top-ranked team in the nation, the UCLA Bruins. Without a doubt, the Cougs would have to bring their A game against UCLA and not let mental mistakes derail them. They could hang with the Bruins, but there would be little room for error. UCLA had an extremely talented roster, led by golden boy quarterback (and Heisman hopeful) Troy Aikman and hard-hitting defensive back Carnell Lake. Both would eventually become All-Pros in the NFL. Through the first seven games of the year, the undefeated Bruins had vanquished the likes of the second-ranked Nebraska Cornhuskers and the sixteenth-ranked Washington Huskies. WSU would be led by Rosenbach (who by then was leading the nation in passing efficiency) and Rich Swinton. They would be without Broussard, who had sprained his ankle the week before against the Sun Devils.

"Anytime you have a player with the impact of Steve missing from the lineup, it hurts you a little," said Erickson the day of the game. "But Richie Swinton is a good player."

Although Erickson gave Swinton high praise, not having Broussard was a difficult prospect for WSU. The Bruins' defense was holding opponents to just 287 yards and 14 points per game. "Nobody has really moved the ball with any consistency against them," Erickson continued. "We're going to have to play flawlessly and the best we've played all year. And then we're still going to have to have some breaks to win the football game."

Even though the Cougars were unranked due to their losses against the Arizona schools, the matchup between two of college football's best quarterbacks was good television and a contest too meaningful to pass up for ABC. The broadcast duo that day included the legend himself, Keith Jackson (WSU class of 1954), along with his partner, Bob Griese. At the beginning of the telecast, Jackson pointed out how UCLA was 4-0 in PAC-10 play while the Cougars were 1-3 and near the bottom of the conference standings. Then Griese compared the programs and quarterbacks, explaining that Rosenbach completed over 70 percent of his passes utilizing the spread formation. Additionally, WSU averaged 38 points per game. Meanwhile, UCLA and Aikman averaged 40 points per game. Both commentators highlighted each team's defense. UCLA was number one in the conference in scoring defense; the Cougars were dead last.

The opening drive started well for Washington State, then fizzled. Fortunately, freshman kicker Jason Hanson kicked a 48-yard field goal straight through the uprights. On UCLA's opening drive, the Bruins looked sharp as Aikman drove the team methodically downfield. At one point, Aikman showed some wheels and scrambled for a huge first-down play. The WSU defense finally held, and Bruins kicker Alfredo Velasco kicked a field goal just over the uprights from 47 yards to tie the game, 3–3. By the end of the first quarter, the game was still tied at 3 and WSU was leading in every offensive category, including rushing yards (36 to UCLA's 29), passing yards (78 to the Bruins' 38) and total yards (114 to 67).

After being stymied in the first quarter, the Bruins got hot in the second quarter. They proceeded to score 17 unanswered points to lead, 20–3. Hanson came on near the end of the quarter and booted a 51-yard field goal, his career-best at the time, to close the gap to 20–6 at the half. By then, it looked like WSU was overmatched. So far, Griese's mention of the difference being the defenses was holding true. In the second quarter, Aikman and running back Eric Ball were wiping the floor with the Cougars, while Rosenbach and WSU could not find the end zone. At one point in the first half, Griese called the contest a mismatch between the two teams. Despite being down by 14 points, Erickson believed the team was still in it. He just asked the team to have a little "Cougar pride" in the second half.

"In our minds, we were like, 'we worked way too hard to be in this position that we're in,'" former Cougars offensive tackle John Husby recalled in 2013. "Where are our leaders at right now?"

Just as the second half began, Griese told the television audience that Rosenbach needed to "play better, avoid sacks, see the blitz coming and know where to go with the football." He also stated that "if Washington State has a chance to win, Rosenbach has to play better." Jackson then added that Rosenbach had some guys open in the first half, "but he simply hasn't hit them." Aikman then proceeded to take the Bruins on an opening-drive score in the third quarter on an 8-yard run by Ball. The score was 27–6 in favor of UCLA. Griese and Jackson hadn't quite written the Cougars off, but many in the crowd did. As the Bruins' lead continued to grow, the number of empty seats in the Rose Bowl increased.

But Rosenbach and the Cougs were not licked yet. After UCLA's touchdown, Rosenbach came alive and threw several crisp passes, including a 15-yard touchdown pass to Stallworth (although video replays clearly showed Stallworth's right knee was down a yard and a half short). The score was now 27–13. On the Bruins' next possession, Ball fumbled, and the Cougars regained possession. Rosenbach began his next offensive possession by scrambling for a couple of first downs. Swinton gashed a huge run and took the pigskin down to the 6-yard line. On the next play, Swinton scored. Suddenly, WSU was down only 27–20. Aikman and UCLA sensed the urgency to increase their lead but didn't capitalize on their next possession. With momentum clearly on their side, the WSU offense poured it on in their next series. After a few plays, Rosenbach found Stallworth for a huge 81-yard catch and run.

"We had a play where I ran a tailback option. We practiced where if they blitzed we hit it quick," said Stallworth.

Jackson noted that the crowd in the Rose Bowl had gotten "very quiet" as Hanson tacked on the extra point to tie the game, 27–27. Television cameras showed the concern on UCLA head coach Terry Donahue's face as the third quarter ended. Aikman and the Bruins had the first possession in the fourth quarter, which led to a 30-yard field goal by Velasco as UCLA reclaimed the lead, 30–27. Rosenbach returned to the field and willed the Cougars into scoring position. "I remember on the sideline when it got down close to the end of the game and guys were saying 'Believe, believe, believe,'" Swinton said in 2013.

With the ball at the 6-yard line, Rosenbach almost ran it in but was stopped at the 1-yard line. On the next play, Swinton scored on a 1-yard dash. With Hanson's extra point, WSU now led number one UCLA, 34–30. WSU kicked off, and the Bruins' return man fumbled the ball as he was tackled, and Hanson recovered it. After the Cougs' offense stalled, Hanson returned to the field but missed wide left on a 36-yarder. Desperation time set in for Aikman and Donahue, but the Bruins' offense moved at a steady pace and eventually worked its way down to the Cougar 46-yard line. On second down, Aikman was intercepted by WSU's Artie Holmes. Aikman's only interception of the game came with 1:59 remaining. WSU then went three-and-out and punted the ball back to UCLA.

Aikman took over with forty-four seconds left after a long return by Darryl Henley. On first down, Aikman hit Charles Arbuckle on a 33-yard pass down to the Cougar 6. With no timeouts left, Aikman grounded the ball on first down. On second down, Aikman's pass to Arbuckle fell incomplete. Third down saw Aikman get hit hard as he threw the ball, which fell incomplete. On fourth and 6 with twenty-six seconds remaining, Aikman's pass into the end zone to receiver David Keating was knocked down by WSU's Vernon Todd. The UCLA crowd was stunned. The Cougars had won the game and the respect of the nation. As the final seconds ticked off the clock, Jackson mentioned how WSU had not beaten UCLA in Southern California since 1958. He also shared how the outcome had to be "one of the most stunning upsets of the college football season."

After the game, Erickson admitted that the victory was the biggest win of his life. Stallworth was named ABC's Chevrolet Player of the Game on the strength of his 7 catches for 170 yards and 2 touchdowns. Rosenbach continued to show why he was one of the best quarterbacks in the country, passing for 272 yards and 2 touchdowns and rushing for 49 additional yards. Swinton ended the day with 117 yards on 27 carries and the game-winning touchdown. As the Cougars peeled off their sweat-soaked uniforms in the locker room, a reporter from an LA newspaper asked Rosenbach what it was like being from Pullman. "Pullman's known mostly for wheat, I guess," Rosenbach replied. "We've got a couple of barbershops, but that's about it. But, hey. I love that town, and I'm just happy to do something like this for them and for Washington State."

Not only were the reporters from the Los Angeles area captivated by this school from wheat country beating their top-ranked team, but the national media also recognized the Cougars' feat as well. *The Sporting News* named Rosenbach its national offensive player of the week.

"We knew if we beat UCLA that we would roll from there because we looked at the rest of our schedule, we were like, 'We got nobody stopping us at this point.' We didn't go down there hoping to win, we were going down there knowing we were going to and we did it," said Rosenbach in 2022.

The Cougars were back on track after their huge victory and were 5-3 as they prepared to head to northern California and face Stanford the following weekend. Shortly after the UCLA victory, Erickson was direct in what WSU had to do to stay alive for a bowl invitation. "What's important for us now is to get that sixth win," he said. "That gives us a winning season, which is what our goal has been like all along. If we can get it this weekend it puts us in great shape coming home for our final two games."

When game day approached, the Cougars were surprised to find themselves as 1.5-point underdogs to Stanford. The expectation by numerous "experts" was that WSU's victory over the Bruins would lead to a letdown in performance by the Cougs.

"Why does there always have to be an emotional letdown?" Erickson asked a reporter. "I've been asked that question so many times I'm sick of hearing about it. This was the best week of practice we've had. If they let down, I'd be so surprised, it would shock the heck out of me."

To be sure, the WSU coaching staff made sure to remind their players of the previous year's loss at the hands of the Cardinal. All week long, the message was clear that there would be no letdown on behalf of the Cougars. Thankfully, the mantra proved true, though just barely, as

WSU escaped California with a 24–21 win to put their record at 6-3. The victory meant that bowl talk was in full swing. By the morning after the Stanford game, everyone knew the stakes. If the Cougs beat Oregon State the following Saturday, it would be very unorthodox if the team wasn't invited to a bowl. Though they tried not to look ahead, the coaching staff and administration considered a number of bowl possibilities and weighed the pros and cons. One option was the Eagle Aloha Bowl. Since it was on Christmas Day, the Aloha Bowl would be the only nationally televised game and give WSU a ton of exposure. Before they could even think about the warm, Hawaiian weather, the Cougars had to square off against the Beavers.

BOWL MANIA WAS IN full swing by mid-November, when 19,702 fans witnessed the Cougs dispatch Oregon State, 36-27. WSU sat at 7-3 and had recently been invited to the Aloha Bowl. In fact, they even knew who they were going to play, the high-scoring Cougars of the University of Houston. It would be the program's first bowl game since 1981. Meanwhile, cross-state rival Washington was experiencing a difficult year and traveled to Pullman for the Apple Cup to play simply for pride. The Huskies were 6-4, and a bowl bid was highly unlikely. Although a year had passed since their 34–19 thumping of the Cougs, Washington had a score to settle with Rosenbach. After the Apple Cup in 1987, Rosenbach told a group of reporters exactly what he thought of the Huskies.

"They have a lot of great dancers on their team. Too bad they can't hit as well as they dance. We're a lot better team than they are. We ran all over those guys today. They were better than us from the 10 in, but that's the only place. I guess that's where it counts, but our program is just as good as their program this year. There, that'll give them some bulletin board material for next year," Rosenbach said.

One year later, Rosenbach was resigned to the fact that the Huskies most likely hadn't forgotten about his statement from the previous season. "I'm sure that stuff's on their bulletin board. I said it and I can't take it back," Rosenbach said. "I know they're going to be fired up and ready to knock my block off. I gotta deal with that when the time comes."

For the first time in fourteen years, the Cougars went into the Apple Cup as favorites. Rosenbach was the number-one quarterback in the nation in passing efficiency, and Broussard led the Pac-10 in rushing and all-purpose yards. Although the team was a little jittery heading into their rivalry game, they were focused on one simple fact. "The driving force going into that game was if we win, they're out," recalled Rosenbach in 2022.

As the contest got underway and large snowflakes began to fall to the artificial turf, the Cougars got on the scoreboard first with a 37-yard field goal by Hanson. Then, calamity ensued as the Huskies scored 3 unanswered touchdowns in the first quarter to take a 21–3 lead. A WSU interception return for a touchdown brought the score to 21–9 to end the quarter. But because of 4 turnovers committed by the Cougars in the first half, Washington took a 28–16 lead into halftime. In the third quarter, Hanson made a 32-yard field goal, and Swinton crashed in from the 1-yard line to edge closer to the Huskies, 28–26. The Huskies kicked a field goal in the fourth quarter to increase their lead to 31–26. They had the ball again a short time later when divine providence appeared to bless WSU.

With 10:42 remaining in the game, Washington punter Eric Canton was in the process of booting the ball when Cougars cornerback Shawn Landrum broke through the line and blocked the attempt. Safety Jay Languein recovered the ball, and WSU was perched on the Huskies' 13-yard line. A short time later, Rosenbach scrambled for 5 yards on fourth and 2 to score and put the Cougars ahead, 32–31, with 9:06 left. Fans from both teams spent the remainder of the contest on the edges of their seats as each side failed to find the end zone. WSU's much-maligned defense came up big and shut down the Huskies on their remaining offensive possessions. Finally, mercifully, the clock showed zeros. The game was over, and the Cougars had won the Apple Cup to finish the 1988 season with an 8-3 record. When the game ended, the WSU faithful went bananas. Erickson was ecstatic. "Our defense in the fourth quarter was flat-out amazing," he said. "Three opportunities, and they just flat shut 'em down."

Rosenbach ended the game completing only 9 passes in 21 attempts for 148 yards and 1 touchdown. He also had 57 yards and 1 touchdown rushing. Broussard left the game in the second half with an injury but contributed 64 rushing yards. Swinton entered in relief for Broussard and ran for 155 yards, his fifth straight game with over 100 yards rushing. He would end the regular season 20 yards short of becoming the Cougars' second 1,000-yard back for the year. As a whole, the Cougars put together 302 total yards on the ground. Though the game got sloppy at times, Rosenbach was ecstatic to beat the Huskies and commented that the victory was bigger than the win against UCLA. "It's a much better feeling beating the Huskies at home when you're supposed to beat them," Rosenbach said.

As the WSU players and coaching staff celebrated in the locker room after the game, Bill Thompson of the Aloha Bowl selection committee was on hand to officially invite the team to Hawaii for Christmas day. "Gentlemen," said Thompson to the Cougars, "I have one question to ask you: How would you like to spend Christmas in paradise?'"

The response was a full-throated roar of acceptance from the Cougs.

BETWEEN THE APPLE CUP and the Aloha Bowl, the Cougars had over a month to prepare their game plan as well as let the accolades wash over them. The fact that WSU would be returning to their first bowl game since 1981 was interesting enough. What was more fascinating was the fact that it would only be Washington State's fourth bowl game in program history. Seemingly out of nowhere, this small school in eastern Washington was making a lot of noise. They were the eighteenth-ranked team in the nation and were about to face the fourteenth-ranked Houston Cougars. The national media couldn't help themselves and paid the Cougars a visit in the weeks leading up to the Aloha Bowl. Rosenbach was widely discussed by football writers for his amazing accomplishments in 1988. He had transformed himself from a player who threw for 2,446 yards, 11 touchdowns and 24 interceptions in 1987 to a focused athlete who passed for 3,097 yards, 24 touchdowns and 11 interceptions and led the nation in passing efficiency in 1988. Rosenbach finished seventh in the Heisman Trophy balloting for the season. Additionally, he ended the season with the Pac-10 record in total offense, edging out John Elway's 1982 conference record with 3,155 total yards to 3,106 total yards. As much as the Cougars tried not to let all the attention get to their heads, they had to admit that it was kind of fun being noticed.

"The fact that we were going to a bowl game, everybody in the college football world was like, 'What the hell's going on in Pullman?' I can remember the magnitude of some of that stuff," recalled Rosenbach in 2022. "ESPN's Chris Fowler actually came out to Pullman and did a little piece on me. And I'll never forget it because they had a shot of me, they wanted a shot of me walking out of the library. And all the boys were out there going, 'You don't even know what that building is.'"

One could also excuse the Cougar players for not fully realizing the magnitude of playing in a rare bowl game. As young men, they were more focused on other aspects of the trip, especially after arriving in Hawaii a week before the contest.

"We knew what we were playing for, but at the same time, we were a bunch of 18, 22-year-old dudes going to go to Hawaii, that's what we were fired up about," Rosenbach added in 2022. "Some of us were probably a little more conscious of that [WSU's rare bowl appearance] than others, but in the same sense, it was like we were trying to figure out how we could get from practice to the beach efficiently and then make it into curfew on time."

Both Cougar squads entered the contest ranked in the top four nationally in offense. WSU was ranked third in the country, averaging 494.4 yards and 35.5 points per game. Houston was fourth with 484.64 yards and 41.1 points per game. While Erickson trotted out his one-back spread offense, Houston coach Jack Pardee was using the run-and-shoot offense. "They're definitely more shoot than run," said WSU's Artie Holmes.

"We're going to play a lot of nickel [five defensive backs] against them," said Erickson. "You have to against that outfit."

Despite Holmes's joke, Houston did boast 1,000-yard rusher Chuck Weatherspoon, who averaged an astounding 8.5 yards per carry and collected 10 touchdowns for the year. The Houston Cougars also played two quarterbacks in 1988, with sophomore Andre Ware getting most of the snaps and senior David Dacus seeing enough playing time to pass for over 1,500 yards. In the days leading up to the game, unpleasantries were exchanged between members of each team. Then, as the game got underway, the chippiness continued.

On the opening kickoff, Houston's James Dixon took the kick and returned it to WSU's 15-yard line. The WSU Cougar defense kept Houston out of the end zone, and kicker Roman Anderson booted a 27-yard field goal to put Houston ahead, 3–0. The remainder of the first quarter was a stalemate, with neither team scoring. Then, in the second quarter, WSU erupted. As the Cougars were driving for a score shortly into the quarter, Broussard fumbled the ball on his way to the end zone. WSU receiver Victor Wood spied the ball, scooped it up and sprinted in for a 7–3 lead. "I'd been blocking back on a defensive back, and I happened to see the ball pop out, so I ran after it," Wood recalled after the game.

Quarterback Timm Rosenbach attempts a pass.

One possession later, Rosenbach found Wood in the back of the end zone for a 15-yard touchdown strike, putting the score at 14–3, WSU. With 6:31 remaining in the half, Hanson kicked a 33-yard field goal to increase the lead to 17–3. Less than two minutes later, Houston's Weatherspoon dashed in from 1 yard out, but the point-after try was missed. WSU now led, 17–9. Rosenbach and company got the ball back and marched down the field again and scrambled for a 1-yard touchdown to put the Cougar lead at 24–9 before halftime.

As the second half got underway, Houston continued to sputter. The primary issue was Ware, who had completed only 8 of his 28 passes for 44 yards and 2 interceptions. Pardee turned to Dacus late in the third quarter, and the senior found receiver Kevin Mason for 53 yards and a touchdown. With the extra point, WSU's lead decreased to 24–15. In the final quarter, Dacus struck again when he found Weatherspoon for a 2-yard touchdown pass that put the score at 24–22. After their touchdown, Houston had plenty of time to find paydirt again. WSU's nickel defense kept the Houston offense from the end zone, and the game ended with the Cougars' ninth win of the year (the most program wins since 1930). Regrettably, the contest ended in a brawl when the constant trash talk from both sides reached a breaking point. On the final play of the game, WSU receiver Michael Wimberly was shoved after the whistle by Houston's Mecridric Calloway. Wimberly shoved back, and fisticuffs ensued.

"They tried to intimidate us the whole game," Wimberly said after cooler heads prevailed. "They never stopped talking, never stopped trying to get to us."

Although the game ended on a sour note, WSU flew back to Washington with their first bowl win since 1915. Despite the hoopla surrounding Houston coming into the game, Rosenbach sliced through the Cougar defense for 306 passing yards, 1 touchdown and 1 interception. Wood was named the Aloha Bowl MVP based on his unexpected contributions, and Broussard led all rushers with 33 carries for 139 yards, both marks Aloha Bowl records.

"There's no doubt in my mind that we play in the best league in the country," Rosenbach said about the Pac-10 after the game. "All I can say is, it sure seems a long way from 3-7-1."

6

TRANSITIONS

I t was only two days after the Aloha Bowl victory, and the Cougars were already looking ahead to 1989. Dennis Erickson had three years left on his contract, and Timm Rosenbach was one of the best college quarterbacks in the nation. The next year would be Rosenbach's senior year, and as far as Erickson was concerned, his quarterback would be returning. "Timm played really well," said Erickson. "He made some real big plays. Let's face it. He's as good as there is in the country. And he's going to be back."

Despite the optimism, events were transpiring in the south of Florida that would soon change the fortunes of both men. For several decades, the University of Miami football team was an afterthought on its own campus. The program rarely posted winning records, and the administration was ready to pull the plug by the late 1970s. Under the direction of coaches Lou Saban and Howard Schnellenberger, the Hurricanes climbed out of the morass. Schnellenberger took the 1983 team to an 11-1 record and an Orange Bowl victory. In 1984, he left the school, and Oklahoma State coach Jimmy Johnson was hired. Five seasons later, Johnson's Hurricane teams had lost just nine games during his tenure and took home the national title in 1987. Miami's 1988 team went 11-1 and barely missed a second straight title.

Just when it looked like Miami and Johnson would continue throttling the competition for many more years, Jerry Jones threw a monkey wrench into their best-laid plans. In February 1989, Jones bought the Dallas Cowboys and fired Tom Landry, the only head coach the organization had ever known. Then, Jones contacted his former Arkansas Razorback teammate, Johnson, and asked if he'd like to become the new coach of the Cowboys. An offer to coach one of the premier franchises in the NFL (despite their recent hard times) and the chance to work for his old friend was too much for Johnson. He signed on the dotted line, and by the last week of February, the Cowboys had a new coach.

Of course, that meant the Hurricanes needed a replacement for Johnson. The Miami faithful were adamant that offensive coordinator Gary Stevens should be elevated to the top spot. After all, he had been with the program for six years and was a good coach. Athletic director Sam Jankovich had other ideas. It just so happened that Jankovich was a Montana native and had played for the University of Montana Grizzlies in the late 1950s. After graduating, he spent several years coaching at the high school and college levels. One of Jankovich's coaching stops was at Montana State University, where the quarterback was—you guessed it—Dennis Erickson. Both men crossed paths through the decades, as Erickson rose through the coaching ranks and Jankovich turned to athletic administration. In 1983, the University of Miami hired Jankovich as its athletic director. Under his direction, the school's teams, especially football, gained prominence.

Enter Erickson. The year 1988 was a special one for the coach. Only a year after naysayers were ready to bury his one-back offense, Washington State had upset the number-one team in the nation and won a bowl game for the first time since 1915. The '88 Cougars became the latest example of what Erickson's offense could do. Major college athletic directors could ignore his talent no longer. Whatever Dennis Erickson was cooking, the big programs wanted a taste.

Jankovich, for one, was already sold. He had seen Erickson's football IQ as an athlete at Montana State. All those years learning the game at his father's elbow put Erickson light years ahead of his teammates in terms of football strategy. Then, as time went on, the two kept in touch, and Jankovich kept an eye on how his former charge was changing offensive football. In Jankovich's opinion, Erickson's one-back spread was the perfect fit for the Hurricanes. The 1989 squad would include such returning players as quarterback Craig Erickson (no relation to Dennis), running backs Leonard Conley and Stephen McGuire and receivers Randal "Thrill" Hill, Wesley Carroll and Dale Dawkins. Erickson's offense paired with the likes of the athletic players Miami boasted gave Jankovich chills. Despite the fact that Erickson wasn't on the radar of the South Florida populace, Jankovich wanted to gauge his interest anyway and reached out to his friend.

Even in 1989, news traveled fast, and the media found their way to Erickson to ask if he was leaving Washington State. It was only a few days after the Cowboys hired Johnson, and Erickson was already denying he was leaving the Cougars. "I'm staying at Washington State. That's what I wanted to do, and I feel very, very much obligated to do that," Erickson said in late February.

For his part, Jankovich didn't push the issue—at first. "Denny is an outstanding coach and an outstanding person," Jankovich said. "But I'm surely not going to visit with anybody that's committed to where they are."

Erickson didn't plan on leaving Washington State. As he told the public at his first press conference, the Cougars really was his destination program. However, the lure of a national title contender was, at the very least, enticing. In the days ahead, Jankovich reached out again, and Erickson rebuffed him again. Finally, after turning down Jankovich twice, Erickson couldn't resist the opportunity to show the world what he and his offense could do. Just days after telling the local media that he had met with Miami only to visit and hear out Jankovich, Erickson became the Hurricanes' new coach on March 5.

"It was an agonizing decision," said Erickson at the time. "I didn't want people to think I'm a vagabond coach. But there was no way I could turn Miami down."

He elaborated in 2022: "It was pretty hard to pass up a place like that when you get a chance to win a national championship. It was difficult though. Difficult on my family. You go from Pullman, Washington, to Miami, Florida."

Unlike his former Wyoming players, many of the Cougars had only good things to say about their coach, even though he had been with the program for only two years. "I think it was based on the opportunity to be able to coach for a national championship every year," said quarterback/defensive back Ron Hawkins. "If you're a coach, that's what you'd want to do. He's got the opportunity and how does he know if he'll ever get it again?"

Running back Rich Swinton mostly agreed with Hawkins. But he was still shocked. "I was a little surprised," said Swinton. "You always hope that he wants to stay, but all week long we've been hearing he was leaving, so you prepare yourself for the worst and hope for the best."

While Erickson was still mulling the offer from Miami, Rosenbach was agonizing about a decision he needed to make. After the Aloha Bowl, Rosenbach was on a perpetual seesaw. He could stay with the Cougars and try to get back to another bowl game in 1989. Swinton and Broussard were coming back, and the three of them could make the Cougars a contender. The problem was that Rosenbach was tired of school. Specifically, he hated the classwork that went with being a college athlete. His teammates were only half joking during his ESPN interview before the Aloha Bowl. He didn't make a habit of using the library to be studious. Additionally, there was no reason to stay in school another year if his father wasn't there to see him play.

"Where I was in my life at that point, my dad had passed away, I hated school. I absolutely hated it," said Rosenbach in 2022.

The NFL had a rule at the time in which the league did not permit certain underclassmen to declare for the draft. The league had made exceptions to the rule, such as allowing Oklahoma State's Barry Sanders, a true junior, to enter the draft in 1989. Rosenbach considered the idea of turning pro a year early. He sought out Erickson and asked his opinion. "I told him that he had a great future and could play in the NFL," Erickson told the *Los Angeles Times* in 1989.

With the blessing of his coach, Rosenbach ultimately decided to turn pro just days before Erickson's own announcement. "I have weighed all the facts and I'm confident that I've done what is best for Timm Rosenbach," Rosenbach said during a press conference in Spokane.

Timm was asked whether Erickson's pending Miami decision and his poor grades had anything to do with his decision, but he denied both. He was adamant that it was time to move on and it had nothing to do with his surroundings or any other factors. "The opportunity is there now," he said. "It has nothing to do with Pullman. Pullman is a great community. It's just time to go on now. I have an opportunity."

Even with his impressive credentials, some NFL personnel strongly believed that Rosenbach needed to stay for his senior year to gain more experience. Gil Brandt, then a respected personnel guru for the Cowboys, thought Rosenbach needed more time for a pair of reasons. "I thought he improved dramatically this year," Brandt said. "I tried to point out to him that if he stayed another year he was going to improve more. Had he waited he would have been drafted higher than he's going to be now," Brandt continued. "He probably will be a player [that will go] toward the end of the first round. After you work him out that may change up or down."

Despite the feedback from NFL evaluators such as Brandt, Rosenbach had made up his mind and was firm in his commitment to leave. "When I signed with Wazzu in 1985, I said…this was my home and there was plenty of time to leave home later," Rosenbach said in 1989. "I feel that this is simply that time."

The reaction to Erickson leaving Washington State wasn't related only to the fact that he still had three years left on his contract. There was also the unpleasant fact, especially for WSU athletic administration, that the Cougs were only weeks away from spring ball. Not having a coach in place at the time sent the wrong message to incoming recruits and high school seniors looking for a college to play football. Athletic director Jim Livengood quickly put together a short list of candidates to replace Erickson. Among them were Jack Elway, former Idaho coach Keith Gilbertson, Ray Dorr (receivers coach at USC) and Mike Price. The hope was that WSU would hire an internal candidate to maintain some continuity in the program. Offensive coordinator Bob Bratkowski's name was mentioned several times as a logical candidate, but Erickson planned to take Bratkowski with him to Miami.

For Price, it must have been torture having his name linked to the job. After he was selected over Erickson to be Weber State's head coach in 1981, Erickson was selected instead of Price for both the Wyoming and Washington State jobs. "I interviewed for the Wyoming job and then he got it, and then when the Washington State job came open, we both interviewed for the job and he got that too," Price reflected in 2022. "And so not only did we face each other on the field, but also in securing jobs."

Price had applied for the open WSU job in the winter of 1976, when coach Jackie Sherrill left after one season. He didn't get the position then, either. In the spring of 1989, Price was once again a strong candidate for the head job. After his Weber State squad went 10-3 in 1987 and advanced to their first playoff appearance in program history, the Wildcats finished the 1988 season 5-6. In eight years at Weber, Price had a 46-44 record. There were a number of WSU fans and alumni who liked the idea of Price returning to Pullman because of his ties to the school and the fact that he ran an offense similar to Erickson's.

After several days of interviews and countless speculation, Price finally got the job he had long wanted. He was officially hired as the Cougars' head coach on March 14. When reached for comment, he couldn't have been more ecstatic. "Washington State has always been my dream job," Price said. "It's going to be difficult leaving Weber State, but I've always picked up the newspaper to see how Washington State did."

Livengood had considered up to eighty candidates, but Price was at the top of the list during the entire process. It helped that Livengood and Price had been teammates at Everett Community College in 1964 and had

Coach Mike Price (*left*) and kicker Jason Hanson.

remained friends. Still, that didn't stop Price from agonizing over the process before the decision was made.

"When the job came open, I said to my wife, 'I think I'm going to apply for that job.' She says, 'No, you don't apply, they should call you. This will be your third time that they shut you down. They should be calling you.' Well, anyway, he [Livengood] didn't call me, he didn't call me, he didn't call me. So he finally called, and I said, 'Damn it, what took you so long?'" Price laughed in 2022. "Anyways, I interviewed with other outstanding candidates, had some real good candidates for that job and felt really lucky to get it."

The outpouring of approval by longtime Cougar alumni regarding the Price hiring was encouraging. Tony Savage, a Cougars player who was part of Livingood's search committee, believed that Price was a good hire while also making a small request. "I think it's a good choice," said the senior defensive tackle, "one of the best choices that could have been made. Basically, he's a coach dedicated to the passing game. I just hope he doesn't change the defense, either."

Even Pinky Erickson chimed in about Livengood's choice of candidates. "Next to Dennis Erickson, they got the best available football coach in the country."

For a brief moment, the announcement that Price was the new coach of the Cougars made Rosenbach question his NFL decision. "I heard Mike was coming in, which made me want to stay because I knew Coach Price; he recruited me out of high school. And I knew him. I knew him since I was a kid. Our families were friends," said Rosenbach in 2022.

The moment passed quickly, and Rosenbach returned to his commitment to becoming a pro. He had carefully considered agents he knew would help him become one of the first quarterbacks taken in the 1989 NFL Draft. Among those who offered to represent Rosenbach was Leigh Steinberg, who represented many NFL players, including Troy Aikman, the likely number-one pick in the upcoming draft. Eventually, Rosenbach chose Gary Wichard, whose client list included Brian Bosworth, the outspoken linebacker from Oklahoma who was drafted by the Seattle Seahawks in 1987. In his pitch to become Rosenbach's agent, Wichard suggested that Rosenbach skip the regular NFL Draft and enter the league's supplemental draft instead.

Implemented by the NFL in 1977, the supplemental draft was a means of entry into the league for players who were not in the regular draft. Before 1990, only college players who had either graduated or finished their eligibility were permitted to enter the draft. There were exceptions made by the NFL (as in Rosenbach's case), and some agents found ways around the rule. Beginning in 1993, the league changed the supplemental draft rules to include players who were unable to attend college, sometimes for disciplinary reasons.

Typically held a few months after the regular draft, the supplemental draft works a bit differently than the main draft. As the NFL states on its website: "Supplemental drafts operate differently than the annual draft, with teams instead submitting bids on prospects based on the round in which they'd like to select a player. If they are awarded the player, they then forfeit their equivalent pick in the traditional draft in the following year."

Not every team participates in the supplemental draft, and many times, the extra draft amounts to only a handful of players being selected (the 1989 version of the draft consisted of five players). More often than not, agents will advise their players to enter the supplemental draft to avoid a team that would pick them in the regular draft or as a means to make better money. Bosworth served as an example. The rebellious linebacker from Oklahoma didn't want to play for the Indianapolis Colts or the Buffalo Bills, two franchises picking early in the regular draft. He hired Wichard, who suggested that "The Boz" use the supplemental draft for maximum dollars and to play for an organization he liked. Bosworth agreed, was selected by the Seattle Seahawks in the 1987 supplemental draft and received a ten-year, $11 million contract, the richest rookie deal in NFL history to that point.

The wheeling and dealing Wichard did for Bosworth was the primary reason Rosenbach decided to hire him. Wichard believed the supplemental draft would be better for Rosenbach, because the agent (and the entire sports world) knew that Troy Aikman would be the first quarterback taken in the 1989 draft. "Gary talked to me about, 'Well, you don't want to go in the regular draft because Troy's going to go first and then you're going to get slotted behind him,'" recalled Rosenbach in 2022. "He said, 'If you go as a first-round pick for the next year, then your present value is going to be greater than his [Aikman's].'"

Also entering the supplemental draft that year was the University of Miami's Steve Walsh. When the time came for the draft, the Dallas Cowboys selected Walsh with the first pick. The move was more than a little surprising, as Dallas had also grabbed Aikman with the first overall selection of the regular draft. Without a doubt, Jerry Jones was committed to turning around the fortunes of the Cowboys. Then, the Denver Broncos submitted a first-round bid and selected Alabama running back Bobby Humphrey. The third pick of the supplemental draft was made by the Phoenix Cardinals, who selected Rosenbach. Essentially, the Cardinals believed in Rosenbach enough that they were willing to forfeit their first-round pick in 1990 for his rights. For his part, Rosenbach was stunned by the selection.

"It didn't make any sense to me," Timm said in 2022. "I thought I was going to the Chargers, even though they had taken Billy Joe Tolliver in the second round, I had a lot of indications that that's where I was going, and then the Cardinals picked me and I was like, 'The Cardinals!?' I never even talked to anybody from there. I knew they were at my workout, but I had never really talked to anybody from the Cardinals that I knew of."

Rosenbach irked Cardinal fans as well as management when he held out of training camp and didn't report until three weeks later. When he did, Rosenbach was confronted by coach Gene Stallings, who was less than pleased. "When I got there and I saw Gene (who I talked to like twice before that), I got my ass ripped for being twenty-one days late to practice," Rosenbach recalled in 2022. "Gene Stallings was that way. It wasn't really a loud ass ripping, but it was a good one."

When the 1989 season began, Rosenbach was buried on the Cardinals' quarterback depth chart behind Gary Hogeboom and Tom Tupa. As Phoenix limped to a 5-11 record, which included the firing of Stallings after eleven games, Rosenbach got on the field for just one start near the end of the year and pass for a total of 95 yards and 1 interception.

Dennis Erickson met his new Hurricane squad in early April 1989, and he used the spring to install his one-back offense. As talented as Rosenbach, Stallworth and Broussard had been for the Cougars, these Miami Hurricanes and their immense talent took to the new offense quickly. Miami ran the one-back to perfection in 1989, losing only once, to rival Florida State. Despite their loss to the Seminoles, the Hurricanes were selected to face seventh-ranked Alabama in the Sugar Bowl on New Year's Day. The game was close until Miami pulled away to win, 33–25. By virtue of Notre Dame beating top-ranked Colorado in the Orange Bowl, the Hurricanes headed home with their third national championship since 1983.

For Dennis Erickson, it must have been surreal. It had been only a decade since he and Jack Elway had tinkered with a new offense they called the one-back. Between 1979 and 1989, Erickson used the offense to inject life into college football. Along the way, he was met with some derision and scoff, but this was the pièce de résistance of what Erickson was trying to accomplish. He had proven that his offense could win at the highest level. With Miami's victory and national title, Erickson's offense became the first purely spread-based offense to win a national title in college football history. He was also the first coach to win the national championship in his first year at a school since Michigan's Bennie Oosterbaan in 1948.

"If somebody had told me seven years ago that I was going to be at a school like Miami and coach the national champions, I'd have never believed them," Erickson told the Spokane *Spokesman-Review*.

While Erickson was at the pinnacle by 1990, Mike Price was navigating the growing pains of taking over a new program. He would find the going bumpy at first, but fortune would soon smile on him and the Washington State faithful.

7

DREW BLEDSOE AND THE 1992 SEASON

ollege football coaches can't spend all their time developing prolific offenses and planning for opponents, as much as they might prefer otherwise. A good portion of their job is devoted to preparing for the future. While they hone the skill set of the players already in their care, coaches are also scouring the country for players who will eventually replace their current lot. The idea is to recruit athletes who can bring the program wins and help the coaching staff keep their jobs. Obviously, when recruiting, the coaching staff is on the lookout for athletes who are capable of playing the sport at a certain level. They can identify talent, but it's another thing completely to find transformational talent. In fact, it's actually quite rare that an athlete comes along who is so uniquely gifted that a coach does everything in his power to recruit said athlete. That's exactly what happened when Mike Price saw Drew Bledsoe for the first time.

Only months after arriving on campus for his new job, Coach Price took a recruiting trip to Spokane, Washington to attend Blaine "Shorty" Bennett's Northwest Football Camp. Bennett was a longtime high school and college coach in Washington, including stops at Ellensburg High School and Walla Walla High School. It was during his years as a high school coach that Bennett met Mac Bledsoe, a football coach in the south-central Washington area. In 1972, Bennett and Bledsoe started the Northwest Football Camp to help train young quarterbacks and receivers. The camp became an annual event and was usually attended by Bledsoe's young son Drew. Both families fondly recall the time when Drew was just a year old and he wandered around the grounds of the camp wearing the alligator shoes of future Pro Football Hall of Fame receiver Fred Biletnikoff.

In the summer of 1989, the Northwest Football Camp was being held on the campus of Whitworth University in Spokane, where Bennett was the head coach. At the time, Drew Bledsoe was looking ahead to his senior year of high school. He had already made a name for himself at Walla Walla High School, where his dad was the offensive coordinator. At six feet, five inches tall and weighing over two hundred pounds, and with a howitzer attached to his right shoulder, the young man from central Washington was drawing attention from college coaches. Coach Price was no different. He had heard about Bledsoe and wanted to see what the fuss was about. Price made his way to Spokane and took a spot on the sidelines to watch Bledsoe warm up and throw some passes. After only a handful of throws, Price's jaw was on the ground and his eyes nearly popped out of their sockets. He had worked with some good ball players through the years, but the sight of Drew Bledsoe was something to behold. Bledsoe's tall frame and powerful arm left the new Washington State coach almost speechless.

"'Oh, my god!' was the only thing I thought of when I watched Drew that day," recalled Price in 2022.

After quickly collecting himself, Price spotted Bledsoe's mother, Barbara, standing on the sidelines not far from him. He made his way over and introduced himself and then made introductions with Mac Bledsoe during a break in the camp. "I went running over there and introduced myself and started buttering them up right from the very beginning," laughed Price.

Price kept in touch with the Bledsoes and, weeks later, was in Walla Walla to help Mac Bledsoe install the one-back offense. The elder Bledsoe was already a fan of the one-back and asked if Price and his coaches would come to show the Blue Devil staff the finer points. "We went down there [to Walla Walla] and helped them, which we would've done for any school had they asked," said Price.

While Price's 1989 Washington State team finished the season 6-5 with quarterbacks Aaron Garcia and Brad Gossen, Drew Bledsoe was powering through a tremendous senior season. He passed for a state-record 509 yards during one game and 490 yards in another. The Blue Devils ended the year 6-3, while Bledsoe threw for 2,560 yards, 25 touchdowns and 6 interceptions and was named to the All-State team. Throughout the fall of 1989, Price and his staff kept up the full-court press in pursuit of their prized recruit. It proved to be a hard sell, because Mac Bledsoe was an alum of the University of Washington and had played for the Huskies. The family had regularly attended Husky games, and at one point in his life, Drew had dreamed about following in his father's footsteps. Price and his WSU staff would not be deterred. They knew that a talent like Bledsoe could turn their program around quickly, and they didn't let a little thing like family tradition or heavy competition stand in their way.

During Bledsoe's official recruiting trip to WSU, Price and the majority of the student body pulled out all the stops. Bledsoe was the only recruit invited, and there was a highlight tape presentation during dinner that was unlike anything the Bledsoe family had seen. Among clips of Bledsoe playing in high school, Price had woven in clips of former Cougars Jack Thompson, Timm Rosenbach and Mark Rypien.

"We blended it all together to the Chicago song 'Inspiration' and put it together in a highlight tape," said Price in 2022. "People had never done anything like that before, and then when he came for his recruiting trip, he was the only recruit. And so we had him and his mom there with us and we had a big dinner, and we had all the coaches there and all the coaches' wives, and we walked in this room and all Drew's pictures all over the wall, big blown up posters from high school."

During dinner, Price reiterated to Mac Bledsoe how much Drew meant to the WSU program. Then, as the highlight film wrapped up in the darkened dining hall, the final scene of the film faded into the Flying B Ranch, which Mac Bledsoe's father owned. Price knew the finishing touch was a hit when he saw Barbara Bledsoe crying. Then, when the lights came up, there was another surprise waiting for the guests of honor. "And we turned on the lights and by golly somehow three sororities had gotten all their girls together and surrounded the room and when the lights went on here these pretty girls were singing the school's fight song," said Price.

As the Bledsoes were leaving campus, a large number of WSU students lined the street to wave goodbye. "They're leaving town and they all rushed the car as we were leaving the building and driving down the street. The fraternities were hanging signs, 'We want you, Drew,' 'We want Drew,' 'Come back, Drew, come back,' and pounded on the car doors as he left," added Price.

All the hard work by Price and his staff paid off when Bledsoe committed to WSU on February 1, 1990. "Washington State is close to my home, and that's important, but I also had a real good feeling about the coaching staff," Bledsoe told the press.

After Bledsoe reported to the Cougars before the fall of 1990, he and Coach Price had a discussion. Price wanted to redshirt him for his first year to give him time to acclimate to college football. Bledsoe, on the other hand, wanted to get in on the action right away and asked Price not to redshirt him. Price agreed, and Bledsoe began the season third on the depth chart behind Gossen, a senior, and Garcia, a sophomore. WSU began the '90 season 2-4, including a loss to USC on October 6. During the game, Price alternated among Gossen, Bledsoe and Garcia. That led to grumbling from the media. The backlash grew even more fierce when Price announced Bledsoe as his starter before the team's seventh game against Oregon State.

"Everybody in the world can second-guess me and by the start of the week, it'll all be over with and we can concentrate on beating Oregon State. That's what our job is," Price told the media at the time of his decision.

That wasn't good enough for some of the local scribes, and one writer, the *Seattle Times*' Blaine Newnham, let Price have it. In a commentary printed two days before the Oregon State game, Newnham called out the Cougars' coach. "Price is putting his credibility and our football sensibility on the line with the machinations surrounding freshman quarterback Drew Bledsoe," Newnham wrote. Newnham also believed that Bledsoe was being forced to prove his worth while also justifying Price's "intuition" if not his job. It was the writer's opinion that, as a freshman, Bledsoe should be hitting the books instead of the field and that Gossen and Garcia weren't being given a fair shake. Furthermore, according to Newnham, Price should have kept Bledsoe's redshirt and given playing time to the guys who earned it.

To be fair, there was some discord in the Cougars' locker room over the quarterback kerfuffle. But Price was vindicated in his decision when NFL personnel members began their rounds of colleges in the fall of 1990 and stopped by Washington State. A number of scouts watched the Cougar quarterbacks during practice, and every one of them stared long and hard at Bledsoe. At one point, a scout sidled up to Price and commented that the local press didn't have a clue what they were talking about. That same scout also confided to Price that, if Bledsoe were available at the time, his team would have no problem drafting him.

Bledsoe further put doubts to rest when he completed 10 of 20 passes for 188 yards, 0 interceptions and 3 touchdowns in a 55–24 pasting of Oregon State. He also ran for a score in his first collegiate start. Although he played well, some media members continued to scoff that Bledsoe had simply beaten a bad team. That just made Price double down. "Drew has by far the best arm on the team," said Price. "We need to get him to understand that he's going to be the leader now. Once he gets those leadership qualities, there's going to be no stopping him."

Drew Bledsoe looks for his running back. *WSU Athletics*.

Bledsoe would start the remainder of the '90 season and pass for 1,386 yards, 9 touchdowns and 4 interceptions as the Cougars went 3-8. In 1991, Bledsoe was the starter for the entire season and helped the Cougars to a 4-7 record while throwing for 2,741 yards, 17 touchdowns and 15 picks. He also led the Pac-10 in total offense.

"It became better his sophomore year, but it took a year for him to really take over the team because we still had some guys who thought they should be playing instead of him," explained Price in 2022. "And they're wrong. I mean, they were just wrong. And they weren't bad quarterbacks, they just weren't as good as this guy was going to be."

As if on cue, Bledsoe would show the rest of the country just how good he was when he took the field for the 1992 season.

The roster for the '92 Cougars was well stocked. There was Bledsoe, who had fully grown into his six-foot, five-inch frame; junior receiver Phillip Bobo; senior receiver C.J. Davis; senior running back Shaumbe Wright-Fair; and a defense that included linebackers Lewis Bush and Mark Fields and defensive lineman Chad Eaton. WSU's schedule that season began with an I-AA opponent, the University of Montana. It should have been a light warm-up for the Cougs, but Bledsoe's uncharacteristic 4 interceptions kept the final score close. The 25–13 Cougar victory was not to the liking of the home fans, who believed WSU should have won by much more. Their confidence was further shaken when WSU escaped Tucson, Arizona, the following week with a 23–20 victory over the Arizona Wildcats. Bledsoe engineered a comeback after the Cougars found themselves in a 17–6 hole in the third quarter. The win was made possible by Price's son Aaron, who kicked a 47-yard field goal with thirty-five seconds remaining. "That's why I married Joyce," joked Mike Price, referring to his son's good genes. "She's got great legs."

After a bye week, Bledsoe and a host of Cougar receivers lit up the scoreboard with a 39–37 victory over Fresno State. Davis caught 8 passes for 125 yards and 2 touchdowns, including the game-winner with forty seconds left. Wright-Fair ran for over 100 yards for the third straight game. Fans at the stadium were treated to a showdown between Bledsoe and Bulldog sophomore quarterback Trent Dilfer, who would eventually play in the NFL and win a Super Bowl in Baltimore. Initially, Bledsoe had a shaky start that saw him overthrow his receivers on a number of passes. He eventually settled down and got the best of Dilfer and Fresno State with 21 completions for 323 yards, 2 passing touchdowns, 2 rushing touchdowns and 0 interceptions. Dilfer completed roughly half his passes for 246 yards, 1 touchdown and 3 interceptions.

On October 3, the Temple Owls came to Pullman, and the Cougars had a feast, winning 51–10. Wright-Fair rushed for 114 yards and 4 touchdowns, Bledsoe passed for 214 yards and 1 touchdown and Davis and Bobo had over 100 yards receiving. WSU was now 4-0 for the first time since 1989, and they were feeling good. The good times continued one week later, when the Cougs traveled to Corvallis and whipped Oregon State, 35–10. By the time 3-2 UCLA arrived for their game in Pullman on October 17, WSU was ranked twenty-second in the country. They also had the best offense in the nation. In the days leading up to the contest, the national media got snarky and claimed that WSU had not defeated any team of substance. That notion was put to rest when the Cougars reached 6-0 for the first time since 1930 with a sound 30–17 win. The game against the Bruins was supposed to be Bledsoe's time to shine and put the Heisman Trophy voters on notice. Instead, his day couldn't have been much worse, as the UCLA defense hounded him into only 9 completions for 108 yards, 1 touchdown pass and 2 interceptions. Meeting with reporters after the game, Bledsoe couldn't have cared less about his stats.

"If we had come out and lost 42–7 or something like that and I had a terrible game, then I'd probably be down about it," Bledsoe said. "In this situation, it's so much fun to win, it doesn't even affect me."

That changed the following Saturday, when the USC Trojans bounced WSU from the list of unbeatens in college football. It was 24–7, USC, before the Cougars clawed back to get within 24–21 with three minutes to play. In the end, it wasn't enough, as the Trojans scored a clinching touchdown in the closing minutes to hand WSU their first loss, 31–21. That dropped the Cougars from thirteenth in the country to ninth. It didn't get much better on Halloween, when the Oregon Ducks handed the Cougs their second straight loss, 34–17.

"Two days ago we were a pretty good football team and everybody was jumping on the bandwagon," said Mike Price after the game. "Even after USC, everybody was still chanting for the Cougars, but we lose one game and not everybody is with us anymore."

In 1991, Oregon had trounced the Cougars, 40–14, and Price hoped the '92 squad would get a little revenge, and he shared that nugget with the media. Unfortunately, the Oregon defense in 1992 kept Bledsoe's contributions to a minimum and left Pullman with a 4-4 record. The Oregon game was marred further by a bench-clearing brawl in the fourth quarter and the fact that players for the Ducks stated they used Price's comments about payback from the previous year to motivate them. "I don't give a damn what they say," Price said after the game when told of the Oregon players' reaction to his comments. "I'm concerned about the Cougars."

On November 7, WSU got back on track, barely, when they beat Arizona State, 20–18, to win their seventh game of the season and rise from number twenty-five to twenty-one in the national polls. Then, fifteenth-ranked Stanford promptly crushed the Cougars, 40–3, a week later in California. The loss erased any hope that WSU would play in the Rose Bowl after the season. Even worse, the 7-3 Cougs would need to defeat cross-state rival Washington in the Apple Cup just to have a chance for a bowl bid. A season that began with so much promise was slowly slipping away.

"It doesn't happen every year around here where you go into the tenth game of the season with a chance to go to the Rose Bowl," Price said after the loss, "and when you don't come through, that's disappointing and discouraging."

Mike Price was heading into his fourth Apple Cup as head coach of the Cougars with an 0-3 record against the Huskies. WSU wasn't given much of a chance in the '92 showdown. Washington was Rose Bowl bound, ranked fifth in the country and boasted a 9-1 record. In the week before the game, Bledsoe was in the news discussing his plans for after the season. Although his junior year wasn't quite shaping up as he expected, NFL commentators still believed he would be one of the first picks in the 1993 NFL Draft. At that point in his collegiate career, Bledsoe had passed for 6,638 yards, more than any Cougar quarterback in program history except Jack Thompson. He was also third behind Thompson and Timm Rosenbach for career total offense with 6,428 yards. Bledsoe pledged that he would wait until the season's conclusion before deciding what to do in 1993.

In the Apple Cup, Bledsoe squared off against Husky signal-caller Mark Brunell. Washington also had formidable athletes in running back Napoleon Kaufman, tight end Mark Bruener, All-American tackle Lincoln Kennedy and all-world defensive tackle D'Marco Farr. To put a little more salt in the wound, the game was in Pullman, but the Cougars were two-touchdown underdogs. Then, as game day began, the home crowd was met with a hefty snowstorm, reminiscent of the flakes that came down during the Apple Cup in 1988. Both teams struggled to find good footing, and the best Washington could do was hold a 7–6 lead at halftime.

Then, things got interesting. As the wind started blowing harder and the snow piled up, the Cougars got hot. Not long after the third quarter began, Bledsoe powered a 44-yard pass into the hands of Bobo, who came down with the catch in the end zone and then crashed into a snowbank. That put WSU ahead, 13–7.

"The crazy thing is," Bledsoe said after the game, "I was actually throwing the damn thing to C.J. [Davis]. I don't know if I 'fessed up to it then or not."

The Cougars weren't done. While the Huskies were slipping and sliding, Bledsoe was connecting with his receivers and Wright-Fair was gashing the Washington defense with huge runs. With 3:57 remaining in the quarter, Wright-Fair rumbled straight up the middle of the field 51 yards for a score that put WSU ahead, 28–7.

The Huskies suddenly looked like a high school JV team. Wright-Fair scored 3 touchdowns and finished the game with 191 yards rushing. Bledsoe had 260 passing yards and 2 touchdown passes. Davis hauled in 7 passes, and his 55 total receptions for the year moved him to fifth on the Cougars' all-time list for receptions in a season. Even more interesting, Davis, along with linebacker Lewis Bush, would become the only two Cougars in program history to play in two bowl games. All told, the offense rolled up 475 yards of total offense on the Huskies. Not to be outdone, the Cougs' defense held Washington to just 267 yards of total offense. WSU won the 1992 Apple Cup (or "Snow Bowl," as it became known) convincingly, 42–23, and improved their record to 8-3. "We took advantage of the conditions and beat them," Bledsoe said after the game.

With the upset, the Cougars were in a much better position to get invited to a bowl game than they had been before the Apple Cup. In fact, Mike

Drew Bledsoe in the Snow Bowl. *WSU Athletics.*

Price already knew the type of bowl game he wanted to compete in. "Is there any bowl where there's snow? We're a pretty good snow team," he said after the game.

Only a day later, the team was officially invited to the Copper Bowl in Tucson, Arizona, on December 29. They weren't exactly thrilled about their opponent. The University of Utah was 6-5, hadn't been to a bowl game since 1964 and seemed a questionable pick as the Cougars' opponent. Even Utah coach Ron McBride was in awe of WSU, especially after what they did to Washington in the Snow Bowl. "I watched Washington State's game with Washington," he said. "They took the Huskies, who I think are an awesome football team, and buried them like they were a piece of crap. I watched it. It wasn't even close, was it?"

The local media guaranteed a Cougar victory over the Utes, with one writer going so far as to declare that WSU would hammer Utah. By the end of the first quarter, the scribes looked like geniuses as the 8.5-point favorite Cougs took a 21–0 lead. Wright-Fair opened the scoring with a 3-yard run, followed by a Bledsoe laser to Bobo for 87 yards (which tied a school record) and another 3-yard run by Wright-Fair to close the quarter. The Utes closed the gap to 21–14 in the second quarter before Bledsoe responded with a

Coach Mike Price calls in a play.

48-yard touchdown to Bobo to put the halftime score at 28–14. Utah then scored 14 unanswered points in the third quarter to tie the game. With under six minutes remaining in the quarter, Aaron Price connected on a 22-yard field goal to put the Cougs up by 3.

The Utes took their next possession all the way to the Cougar 2-yard line with just over three minutes to go in the contest. Instead of trying to punch in a go-ahead touchdown, McBride made a questionable decision to go for the tie and kick a short field goal. The notion hardly seemed like a good idea, as Utes kicker Chris Yergensen already had a field goal and point-after try blocked during the game. Sure enough, Yergensen shanked the 20-yard try, and WSU held on for the 31–28 victory. The win was Washington State's third bowl victory in team history and the second in five years. Their 9-3 final record was also identical to Dennis Erickson's Aloha Bowl team in 1988.

"It's really the kids," said Mike Price. "I think this team is special."

Bobo had a big day, finishing with 7 catches for 212 yards and 2 touchdowns. Wright-Fair added 123 yards on 28 carries and 2 scores. He ended the '92 season with 1,331 total rushing yards. Then there was Bledsoe. If there were any questions regarding his pro potential before the game, they were gone now. He passed for a school-record 476 yards and 2 touchdowns and was named the Copper Bowl MVP. Bledsoe also threw for a program-record 3,246 yards for the season, along with 20 touchdowns and 15 interceptions.

"I didn't realize the numbers were that big," Bledsoe said after the game. "But it's easy when you throw short passes to Phillip Bobo and he breaks them."

Now Bledsoe had a decision to make. As The Clash once sang, would he stay or would he go? He had played three years in Pullman and passed for 7,373 yards, 46 touchdowns and 34 interceptions. It didn't seem like there was anything left for Bledsoe to prove in college. On the day of the Apple Cup in late November, Mac Bledsoe made a comment to the Spokane *Spokesman-*

Review that possibly foretold his son's anticipated decision. "Washington State was a great choice for Drew," Mac said. "He's benefited from the experience and exposure of playing early. We appreciate Mike Price. He's a reasonable man in an unreasonable world."

On January 4, 1993, Bledsoe finally made the choice that most of the free world expected. "I want to take my skills to the next level and see how I can do playing football at the highest level," the twenty-year-old said of his decision.

The signal-caller mentioned during his press conference that the lure of staying in college another year and possibly becoming WSU's first Heisman winner did give him pause. Inevitably, playing against the world's best football players and making obscene amounts of money led to his decision. "I've been involved in football for as long as I can remember," said Bledsoe. "And to think somebody would pay me money to play seems almost ridiculous, somehow. Anybody who would pay me to play football, I could play for."

Almost four years had passed since Mike Price first laid eyes on Drew Bledsoe. Now he was leaving for the NFL, and Barbara Bledsoe was a little sad that her son's coach would no longer be Price. "He is everything a mother could ever want in the way of a coach for her son. I have tremendous regard for him as a coach and a person. I just wish Mike Price could go with Drew, then I'd feel just fine. I wouldn't worry at all."

During his press conference announcing his decision to forgo his senior year, Bledsoe told the press he preferred to stay in the Pacific Northwest to play pro football, specifically with the Seattle Seahawks. As the 1993 NFL Draft approached, it looked like that might be a possibility, as the Seahawks had the second overall selection. But Rick Mirer of Notre Dame was another hot quarterback prospect and looked to compete with Bledsoe for the top spot. When the draft got underway, the New England Patriots had the first pick, and many believed they would select Mirer, who reminded people of San Francisco 49ers legend Joe Montana. Instead, New England surprised many, including their own fans, and grabbed Bledsoe.

"In the final analysis, we thought Bledsoe had a little more ability to throw the ball effectively," said Patriots head coach and general manager Bill Parcells.

With the second overall pick, the Seahawks selected Mirer. In the fourth round, the San Diego Chargers drafted WSU's Lewis Bush, and Cougs' tight end Clarence Williams went to the Denver Broncos in the seventh round. Soon after Bledsoe's selection was made, Parcells cautioned Patriot fans not to expect the WSU star to start right away. That was something that Bledsoe hoped to change as a rookie. "I'm a competitor," Bledsoe said. "You always want to be on the field. I haven't been in a situation where I've been on the sidelines a whole lot."

Sure enough, as New England wallowed through a 5-11 season in 1993, Bledsoe started twelve games and passed for 2,494 yards, 15 touchdowns and 15 interceptions. The following year, the Patriots returned to the playoffs for the first time since 1986. Bledsoe led the NFL in several passing categories, including passing yards (4,555). Two seasons later, Bledsoe threw for over 4,000 yards and 27 touchdowns to help lead New England to Super Bowl XXXI in just his fourth year. During the title game, he would stake the Pats to a 14–0 first-quarter lead, only to watch as the Green Bay Packers and quarterback Brett Favre came roaring back to win the game, 35–21. Bledsoe finished the contest with 253 passing yards, 2 touchdowns and 4 interceptions.

8

RYAN LEAF AND A RUN FOR THE ROSES IN 1997

t was January 1, 1994, and Ryan Leaf was watching the Rose Bowl at his parents' house in Great Falls, Montana. The phone rang, and Ryan's mom, Marcia, answered it. The caller wanted to speak to Ryan, and Leaf grabbed it while still watching the game. Seconds later, he was talking to Coach Mike Price of Washington State University. The two made chitchat and discussed the Rose Bowl. Out of the blue, Price said something to Leaf that ultimately led to the biggest decision of the young quarterback's life.

"Ryan, I'll make you a deal," said Price in *596 Switch*, written by Leaf. "If you come to Washington State, you and I will play in that game together."

It turned out that Price was actually at the Rose Bowl that day when he had the idea to call Leaf. "I was at the Rose Bowl game when he was a senior in high school, and I went out to the pay phone booth and stood in line and then called him on the phone," said Price in 2022.

Up to that point, Leaf had been wooed by the likes of WSU, Colorado State, Colorado, Oregon and several other schools, including Dennis Erickson and the University of Miami. Leaf was a standout at Charles M. Russell High School in Great Falls and had the prototypical quarterback size (six feet, five inches and over two hundred pounds) and a powerful arm. He led C.M. Russell to the Montana Class AA state championship in 1992 and led the school back to the playoffs in 1993 before they were eliminated. Not only was Leaf gifted on the gridiron, but he was also a basketball stud. He was an all-state and all-conference selection and team MVP his senior year. Remarkably, Leaf was never honored with an all-state designation for football.

Just before his senior year in 1993, Leaf received a letter in the mail from WSU. He had appeared on the program's radar after attending a football camp in California during the summer of '93. That's where he met the son of Washington State athletic director Jim Livengood. Livengood's son mentioned Leaf to his father, who in turn talked to Mike Price. The letter was more of an introduction, but Leaf was intrigued. The Cougars had a fairly recent tradition of good quarterbacks, including Jack Thompson, Mark Rypien, Timm Rosenbach and Drew Bledsoe. After learning more about Price's spread offense, Leaf and his father, John, took off for an informal visit to the WSU campus. They wanted to watch a Cougar game for themselves and arrived in Pullman on a Saturday to see if the program would be a good fit for Leaf's talents. The trip proved fortuitous, as the Cougs hammered the visiting Oregon State Beavers, 51–6. Actually, it wasn't so much the score that Leaf was enamored of. It was the fact that WSU's quarterback that day, Mike Pattinson, attempted 41 passes. For someone who really enjoyed throwing a football, that stat alone greatly intrigued Leaf.

By the time Leaf's senior football season was ending, he had narrowed his list of prospective schools down to a half dozen, including WSU and Miami. He took an official visit to Pullman and had a fun time with members of the team. On the final day of his trip, Leaf was offered a scholarship by Price. There was no doubt that Leaf enjoyed Pullman and the atmosphere at WSU. He had already learned that the Cougars had a special program that held a place in the hearts of the people who both attended the university and played for the sports teams. "Once a Coug, always a Coug," was a saying among the alumni, and Leaf couldn't get it out of his head. He still had a few more trips to take, though, and he wanted to see what else was out there before making his decision.

Next on Leaf's itinerary was the University of Miami. He didn't actually think he would attend the school, especially since Leaf thought he would be an odd duck going from rural Montana to the bright lights of Miami. However, there was already a Montana connection in place with Dennis Erickson as the head coach. There was also the prospect of playing for a team that had won two national titles under Erikson. During his time in Miami, Leaf saw the sights with Bryce Erickson, Dennis's son, who was a redshirt freshman quarterback for the Hurricanes. Leaf also had a memorable evening hanging out with 'Canes players Warren Sapp and Dwayne Johnson. A few years later, Johnson would wrestle professionally as "The Rock" and become one of the biggest (literally) action stars in Hollywood. Sapp became a dominating defensive player for the Tampa Bay

Buccaneers and helped the franchise win a Super Bowl. During the raucous evening, Leaf got caught up in the nightlife and frivolity and blurted out that he was going to become a member of the Hurricanes. The announcement was greeted with cheers, although Leaf immediately knew that his pledge was not entirely true.

"I was like a cheap imitation of Arthur, spouting off at the mouth about stuff I had no intention of doing," wrote Leaf in his book, referring to the Dudley Moore character in the movie *Arthur*.

The following day, he met with Dennis Erickson and had a candid conversation. Erickson loved Leaf's athleticism but admitted that he wanted to turn Leaf into a tight end. This wasn't a knock on Leaf's ability. Miami already had a full quarterback room, and Erickson needed a tight end. He believed Leaf's size would be a boon for the Hurricanes' passing game. Leaf understood that Erickson was planning ahead from a personnel point of view, but he had no plans to play anything but quarterback. Erickson also admitted that he had designs on becoming an NFL coach. Specifically, if the Seattle Seahawks job opened up, he would jump at the chance. Despite the comment about a possible conversion to tight end, Leaf liked Erickson's frankness and the fact that he wasn't telling Leaf everything he wanted to hear. Still, by the time he returned to Montana, Leaf knew he wouldn't attend Miami.

It wasn't long after the Florida trip that Mike Price called Leaf on New Year's Day 1994. After hanging up, Leaf was overcome with the idea of becoming a Cougar. He told his parents that he was committing to Washington State and would sign his letter of intent. Leaf then called the coaches and recruiters from the schools he wouldn't attend and had an odd conversation with Mike Bellotti, the head coach of the Oregon Ducks. Unhappy with Leaf's decision to attend WSU, Bellotti told him in no uncertain terms that the Cougars would never play in the Rose Bowl and that Leaf would never beat his Ducks. Leaf was shocked at Bellotti's hostility and harbored bitterness toward the coach and the Ducks for many years afterward. The conversation with Bellotti notwithstanding, Leaf was still sold on Washington State and Coach Price. On Signing Day, February 2, 1994, Leaf faxed his letter of intent to Price and the WSU staff. He was now officially a Cougar.

While Leaf rode the pine in 1994 and served as nothing more than a practice arm, the Cougars were experiencing a bit of an anomaly that season. WSU sophomore quarterback Chad Davis had a decent year, passing for 2,299 yards, 10 touchdowns and 6 interceptions. That was

Mike Price on the sidelines.

pedestrian for the spread offense but kept the Cougars in some games. The defense, on the other hand, was hands down one of the best in college football. Nicknamed the "Palouse Posse," they tore through opponents in '94 to become the second-ranked defense in the nation. Only two years after winning a bowl with Drew Bledsoe, the Cougars went 8-4 in 1994, which included a tight 10–3 win over Baylor in the Alamo Bowl. None of the players realized it at the time, but after only six years on the job, Mike Price had qualified for and won two bowl games. No other coach in WSU history had achieved such a feat.

In 1995, Leaf finally experienced his first collegiate game, against the University of Montana in the final quarter, throwing a touchdown pass. His first start came in the Apple Cup in November, a close 33–30 loss to the twenty-second-ranked Huskies. The following year, Leaf was ready to play as the starter. Before the first game of the year against the fifth-ranked University of Colorado Buffaloes, Leaf predicted a huge upset. The Buffaloes took him to task for the prediction and blistered the Cougs, 37–19. Sufficiently humbled but still full of confidence, Leaf went back to work and led the team to five wins in their next six games. WSU then lost their final four games, including a 7-point loss in overtime to the Huskies in the Apple Cup (the first overtime in the series' history). A season that began with a 5-2 record ended in a 5-6 embarrassment. There was a general feeling from Coach Price, the players, local media and fans that the Cougars had underperformed in 1996 and let a good thing slip through their fingers. Without a doubt, 1996 gave Ryan Leaf the motivation to shock the world in 1997.

One of the primary reasons for Leaf's optimism in '97 was the Cougars' roster. It was a testament to Mike Price and the attention the one-back brought to the Palouse that a large number of talented players were now making their way to tiny Pullman. In addition to Leaf, WSU had receivers Chris Jackson, Nian Taylor, Shawn McWashington, Shawn Tims and Kevin McKenzie, otherwise known as the "Fab Five." Then there were the road graders in linemen Jason McEndoo, Ryan McShane, Cory Withrow, Lee Harrison and Rob Rainville, who were appropriately nicknamed the "Fat Five." Senior running back Michael Black was no joke, and the defense had hard-core leaders in seniors Leon Bender and Dorian Boose and a dynamo in sophomore linebacker Steve Gleason. Should their potent offense have to settle for field goals, the very competent Rian Lindell could kick straight and true.

Initially, the Cougars were set to begin their '97 season on September 13 against USC. That changed when Coach Price made a deal with UCLA and ABC Television to move their originally scheduled contest from November to August 30. The change meant that the WSU-UCLA game would be one of the first college football contests of the season as well as nationally televised. Washington State alum Keith Jackson was in town to call the game, which only legitimized the stakes of the contest. Essentially, the Cougars would have to win their first two games of the year against two good California schools. Depending on the outcome, WSU could either be bowl contenders or dead in the water. As the local press mentioned, whenever WSU started a season 0-2 (which had happened sixteen times), they failed to finish the season with a winning record. Also, it mattered not that UCLA had gone 5-6 in 1996. The Bruins owned a 33-11-1 lead in the head-to-head series.

Thankfully, Leaf and the Cougs didn't care about history. The Bruins played well, but their defense had a difficult time keeping up with Leaf and his receivers. Nian Taylor caught 5 passes for 200 yards, and Leaf found numerous holes in the UCLA secondary on the way to 381 passing yards and 3 touchdowns. The Cougs held on to win a close one, 37–34, to start the 1997 season 1-0. After the game, defensive tackle Leon Bender (who was known to spice things up a bit on and off the field) commented to the media how UCLA was a place where players go to become soft. Learning about his player's comment sometime later, Price rolled his eyes and laughed. "I haven't talked to 'Coach Bender' yet, so I'll have to wait until I get his comment on the situation," laughed Price.

The benefit of playing so early in the season was that the Cougs had a bye week before playing in Los Angeles against USC. That gave injured players, Leaf included, time to heal and an opportunity to work out any kinks in the game plan. In the week leading up to the game, the national media was quick to point out that WSU had not defeated the Trojans in Southern California since 1957. Good for the Cougars beating UCLA, but their undefeated season would end against USC, or so the thinking went. One week prior to playing the Cougs, USC lost a close game to fifth-ranked Florida State, 14–7. Before that game, Trojan backup quarterback John Fox made a statement that raised the blood pressure of the WSU team. "I hate losing. If we do lose [to Florida State], we'd have to kill Washington State," said Fox. "Take it out on them."

Fox's declaration required a retort from defensive end Dorian Boose. "I was really bothered about the quote. You know, a guy who's only played maybe three downs of college ball in his life....So I think everybody's kind of excited about that."

They were excited indeed. Leaf passed for 355 yards, 3 touchdowns and 2 interceptions as the Cougars moved to 2-0 after beating the Trojans in their own building, 28–21. It was the first time in program history that WSU beat UCLA and USC in the same season. The highlight of the afternoon was an incredible catch by Kevin McKenzie and a vicious block by Shawn McWashington to enable McKenzie to reach the end zone. It is a play still mentioned in reverent tones among Cougar fans to this day. After the game, Leaf was excited about the win. He enjoyed the fact that the Cougs were ranked in the top twenty-five for the first time in three years. He was also very focused on the task at hand. "The biggest game in the world to me right now is Illinois next week," Leaf said.

On September 20, the Cougars traveled to Champaign, Illinois, and took down the Fighting Illini, 35–22. Leaf was a tad shaky after throwing 3 interceptions, but he turned things around to finish with 302 yards and 4 touchdown passes. Boise State arrived at Martin Stadium on September 27 and was chewed up and spit out, as the Cougs blanked the Broncos, 58–0. WSU was now sitting at 4-0 and became the only unbeaten team in the Pac-10.

Besides the Washington Huskies, there was perhaps no opponent Ryan Leaf loved facing more than the Oregon Ducks. After Mike Belotti's tirade against Leaf's college decision in the spring of 1994, Leaf had made it his mission to make Belotti eat crow. He didn't play in the 1994 game against the Ducks but was still thrilled when the Cougs beat Oregon, 21–7. In 1995, the Ducks roughed up WSU, 26–7. As the starter in 1996, Leaf passed for 225 yards, 4 touchdowns and 1 interception in a 55–44 high-scoring win over Oregon. He continued his streak on October 4, when WSU went to Autzen Stadium in Eugene, Oregon, to face the Ducks. Leaf found the footing that day difficult, as he was held to 226 yards, 1 touchdown and 1 interception. It didn't matter, as the Cougars still won the game, 24–13, to move to 5-0 and a thirteenth overall ranking in the nation.

The Oregon game is also noted for an incident that occurred between a group of Cougar players and Oregon fans sitting behind the WSU bench. For much of the contest, some Ducks fans nearest the Cougs began spewing hateful and racist remarks toward running back Michael Black. As mentioned in Leaf's book, it just so happened that one of the WSU linemen, Cory Withrow, had to relieve himself, and there was no time to get to the locker room to do so. A number of Cougar players shielded Withrow with towels, and he urinated into a Gatorade cup right there on the sidelines. At that moment, the fans began yelling racial slurs again, and Leaf took matters into his own hands, literally. He grabbed the cup full of Withrow's urine, nonchalantly walked over to the unruly fans and proceeded to dump the contents onto their laps. Once they realized what was in the cup (and now in their laps), the Duck fans lost their minds and grabbed an usher to tell him what happened. There wasn't much the usher could do, however. It wasn't like he could escort members of the opposing team out of the stadium. The entire incident would become a footnote in history, as neither the fans nor the Cougar players were reprimanded for their behavior.

Leaf's personal vendetta against Belotti had another unintended effect in 1997. Now that the Cougs were undefeated, recruiting had kicked up to a fever pitch, something that greatly excited Price. "The recruiting phone calls are a lot better now," said Price. "We just have to keep it going through the season."

WSU's perfect record and high-flying offense meant that athletes from all over the country wanted to come to Pullman, Washington. The Cougars had another bye week following the Oregon game, but Price and his staff spent the week visiting with recruits and evaluating the next crop of Cougars. A coach's work is never truly done.

After their bye week, WSU faced the Cal Golden Bears and Arizona Wildcats in consecutive weeks. Leaf, at this point ranked number one in the

Left: Quarterback Ryan Leaf in action during the 1997 season. *WSU Athletics*.

Right: Quarterback Ryan Leaf scrambling for a first down against Cal during the 1997 season. *WSU Athletics*.

country in passing efficiency, battered Cal for 332 yards and 5 touchdowns. He then took apart Arizona with a career-high 384 yards, 3 touchdowns and 1 pick. Both games were wins for the Cougs (the Arizona game was won on a last-second WSU tackle in overtime), and they were now ranked tenth in the country. It was only the third time in WSU's history that the program had been ranked that high. Additionally, the last time the Cougars were 7-0 to start a season was 1930, Babe Hollingbery's Rose Bowl year. Was that a foreshadowing of things to come?

Any talk of going undefeated in 1997 ended on November 1. WSU traveled to Tempe to face the Arizona State Sun Devils and were humiliated, 44–31. Leaf passed for a new career-high 447 yards along with 3 touchdowns (which broke the WSU record for total touchdown passes in a career) and 1 interception, helping his team overcome a 24–0 hole, but it was not enough. After the game, Price was despondent. "I've been here 18 years [as a player, assistant and head coach], and these guys have overachieved many times to get to this point," Price began, "and to get to this point and come up short is just one of the most disappointing moments of my career."

The Cougars took out their frustrations a week later against lowly Southwestern Louisiana. The Ragin' Cajuns never stood a chance in Martin Stadium and lost, 77–7. Leaf hung 305 yards and 4 touchdowns on the Cajuns in limited playing time. WSU then kept their Rose Bowl hopes alive with a 38–28 victory over Stanford on November 15. As he was walking off the field, Leaf struck a little Heisman pose. Normally, that kind of enthusiasm would get a stern rebuke from a coach. Price believed otherwise. "Ryan said it was kind of selfish, but gosh, it was fun," Price said. "And isn't that kinda what it's about? Sometimes we take everything so seriously that, boy, a guy can't relax for just a second. That was kind of refreshing to see."

Talking to reporters after the Cardinal game, Cougars receiver Chris Jackson dispensed high-quality bulletin board material as he looked ahead to the regular season finale against the Huskies. "I'll be damned if I'm going to let the Huskies get in my way of going to the Rose Bowl," said Jackson. "I think they have talented players just as everyone does," he continued, "but I don't have much respect for them as people or as players. I just want to go in there, study film on them and go do what we set out to do, go in and kill them."

Jackson's bravado most likely did not sit well with Price, who preferred not to give his opponents extra motivation. He already had to censor Bender after the defensive lineman had become so sassy in the media that it had become a distraction. That didn't seem to be the case with Jackson's declaration. Instead, his words fueled the Cougars even more in preparing for their cross-state rival.

No doubt about it, Apple Cup '97 promised to be a good one. The Cougars entered the contest as Pac-10 champions (the first time in program history) based on their 9-1 record and were ranked eleventh in the nation. Washington had been cruising along at 7-1 before losing two straight to Oregon and UCLA. Entering the Apple Cup, they were 7-3 and ranked sixteenth nationally. Yet the oddsmakers still favored the Huskies by a touchdown.

It was hard for the Washington State players not to look ahead to a possible trip to the Rose Bowl should they beat the Huskies. In a chat with reporters midweek, Leaf mentioned how he wanted to face the undefeated Michigan Wolverines should WSU make it to Pasadena. "I would want to go up against the best," Leaf said. "It would be a good challenge and a great game."

First things first, as WSU actually had to play a game before they could even think about roses. By the end of the first quarter, Cougars fans shifted uncomfortably in their seats as their team was down, 7–0. The squirming quickly turned to dancing as WSU reeled off 17 unanswered points in the second quarter to take a 17–7 lead into halftime. In the third quarter, the Huskies had 3 touchdowns to WSU's 2, but the Cougs were still ahead by a slim 31–28 margin. The final quarter was a battle to the end, with the Cougars outscoring Washington, 10–7. When the clock displayed all zeros, the scoreboard showed that WSU had beaten their rivals, 41–35. It was the first win for the Cougs in Husky Stadium since 1985.

The euphoria at the final whistle cannot be adequately described. Bedlam and delirium overtook Cougar fans as they fully realized what had just happened. WSU last qualified for the Rose Bowl during the Great Depression. On this day, there was no depression in sight for those cheering for the scarlet and gray.

"There was a little mist on the field, it started to rain a little bit," Price recalled at a ceremony for the twenty-five-year reunion of the team in October 2022. "(Shawn McWashington) somehow was quoted saying, 'That's not rain, that's tears from all the Cougars that are in heaven crying because they're so happy we finally got to the Rose Bowl.'"

Reporters busily typed out the Cougars' stats for the day, still overcome by the fact that they were witnessing something special. Leaf had passed for 358 yards, 2 touchdowns and 1 interception and had also run for a score, cementing his Heisman bid. Motormouth Jackson, who had defied a Husky victory before the game, caught both touchdowns from Leaf while accumulating 185 yards. Michael Black, the Cougs' maestro running back, tallied 170 yards and 1 touchdown. Freshman defensive back Lamont Thompson was Johnny-on-the-spot, as he collected no less than 3 interceptions. "This football team will be remembered for 100 years," said Price after the game.

As he stood on the field amid his teammates, Leaf realized that Price's Rose Bowl promise to him on New Year's Day 1994 had come true. He also understood what a Rose Bowl berth meant to Cougar fans and the Pullman community. "It's hard for me to believe it's been that long [sixty-seven years since WSU's last Rose Bowl appearance]," said Leaf. "I understand what they (Cougar fans) have been waiting for. I've only been waiting for three years.

Leaf finished the 1997 regular season as the Pac-10 single-season passing leader as well as WSU's single-season passing yardage king. He was named the Pac-10 Offensive Player of the Year, Pac-10 Conference first-team offense and *The Sporting News* first-team All-American. Coach Price was recognized for his leadership by being named Pac-10 and National Coach of the Year.

A few weeks later, the entire Leaf family, as well as Mike and Joyce Price, were in New York City for the Heisman Trophy presentation. Leaf had stiff competition for the coveted award, along with finalists Charles Woodson of Michigan and University of Tennessee quarterback Peyton Manning. The Leaf clan had their pictures taken with the award and good times were had by all. In the end, Woodson was named the Heisman winner, and Leaf finished third in the voting behind Manning. All was not lost, however. Leaf won the Columbus Touchdown Club's Sammy Baugh Passer-of-the-Year award.

Leaf got his wish. The Cougars would be facing the University of Michigan Wolverines on New Year's Day for the Rose Bowl. The Wolverines were undefeated and ranked number one in the country. The program also boasted the newly minted Heisman Trophy winner in Woodson. Michigan averaged 26.8 points per game and gave up less than 100 points for the entire regular season. Their quarterback was All-Big Ten selection Brian Griese, son of former Miami Dolphin Bob Griese. Blocking for Griese was guard Steve Hutchinson and tackle Jon Jansen, both also All-Big Ten selections. Griese occasionally passed to Woodson, who played on both sides of the ball. The Michigan defense had no less than five All–Big Ten members. (On a side note, one of the Wolverine clipboard holders that day was sophomore quarterback Tom Brady, the same Tom Brady who would win seven Super Bowls in the NFL.)

On the other side of the field were the Cougars, ranked eighth in the nation. WSU averaged 40.2 points per game, although the defense gave up over 200 points for the '97 season. Essentially, it was the Cougs' second-ranked offense versus Michigan's top-ranked defense. The two programs had only one loss between them, but the national media didn't give the Cougs much of a chance. This was, after all, the mighty Wolverines, and they were facing Washington State, the school located in wheat country. Sure, the Cougs had Leaf, but how good could they really be? All that talk was nonsense to Jack Neumeier. The man who started the spread offense with a young John Elway and taught that offense to Jack Elway and Dennis Erickson believed in the Cougars. "I want to tell you, if Washington State is doing (my offense) properly, it'll kill Michigan with it," Neumeier said three days before the game.

By game day, the betting line had returned to Earth, and Vegas had installed Michigan as 7.5-point favorites. After the contest began, the Cougars clearly showed that they were not intimidated and took a 7–0 lead on a Leaf pass to Kevin McKenzie for 15 yards. The touchdown was only the third

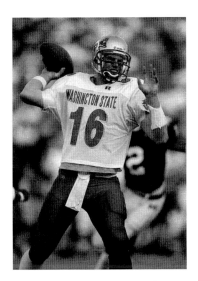

Quarterback Ryan Leaf in action during the 1998 Rose Bowl against top-ranked University of Michigan. *WSU Athletics.*

one allowed in the first quarter all season by the Michigan defense. In the second quarter, Griese found receiver Tai Streets for 53 yards and a touchdown to tie the score, 7–7, going into halftime. Michigan opened the second half by driving down to the WSU 37-yard line before the Cougars held. Leaf then calmly took his mates on a long drive before receiver Shawn Tims scored on a 14-yard reverse. One play later, the Wolverines' James Hall blocked WSU's extra-point attempt, which kept the Cougars' lead at 13–7.

Michigan then used their next possession to flex a little muscle, and Griese found Streets again for a huge 58-yard touchdown and 14–13 advantage. In the fourth quarter, the Wolverines took their time and chewed up the clock on a 14-play possession that took over five minutes. Griese spotted tight end Jerame Tuman for 23 yards and a 21–13 lead. WSU could muster only a 48-yard field goal by Rian Lindell on the ensuing drive to cut the Michigan lead to 21–16. The Wolverines then took over and purposely took their time on offense and ran the clock down to twenty-nine seconds. After punting the ball back to WSU, the Cougars took over at their own 7-yard line with seemingly no hope left.

Leaf wasn't done yet. Two quick passes resulted in 0 yards, and then there was a delay of game penalty. Out of the depths of despair, Leaf connected with Nian Taylor for a 46-yard gain. On the next play, Leaf found Love Jefferson on a pass, and Jefferson promptly lateralled to Jason Clayton for a shocking 36-yard play. That put the Cougs at the Michigan 26-yard line with two seconds left. Price signaled in "596 Switch" (hence the title of Leaf's book). The offense had worked on the play repeatedly in practice, and it promised good returns if executed correctly. Leaf tried to spike the ball on the next snap to stop the clock. To his dismay, Leaf heard the referee blow his whistle and signal that the game was over.

The Washington State sideline went ballistic. In their opinion, there was no way two seconds had elapsed before Leaf spiked the ball. While Price tried to state his case, Leaf ran after the officials to plead for more time. ABC, which was covering the game, examined the replay. The tape clearly showed that one second remained when the ball touched the turf. In fact, referee Dick Burleson had signaled for the clock to stop with that exact amount of time remaining. Before time could freeze, the game clock expired. Burleson then changed his mind and signaled for the end of the game. Price acknowledged later that having one more play didn't necessarily mean that WSU would score the game-winner. He just thought the team should have been given the opportunity to do so.

"Everyone knows you can down the ball with less than two seconds left on the clock," Price said. "The officials made a mistake, I think. The fact is, we still have to make a play there to win it. But it would have been nice to go out and try it."

Leaf's take on the controversy was simple. "It stinks," he said.

The NCAA reviewed the matter during the following week and agreed with Burleson's ruling. "If the clock stops because of a first down, the referee restarts the game clock as soon as the chains are in place and the officiating crew is in position," said John Adams, secretary editor of the NCAA football rules committee, referring to Rule 3-2-5 of the NCAA's football rule book. "In this case it appeared there were two seconds remaining when he restarted the clock by winding it, and according to his discretion, no time remained on the clock by the time the ball was spiked."

Dejected and worn out, the Cougars made their way back to the locker room. Their amazing season ended 26 yards from glory, but the team knew they had given it their all. Griese was named MVP of the Rose Bowl. Streets caught 4 passes for 127 yards and 2 touchdowns. Leaf completed 17 of 31 passes for 331 yards, 1 touchdown and 1 interception. For the 1997 season, he passed for 3,968 total yards along with 34 touchdowns and 11 interceptions. Michael Black led the team in rushing with 1,181 yards and 12 total scores, and Chris Jackson led in receiving with 1,005 yards and 11 touchdowns.

ONE DAY LATER, LEAF held a press conference to announce that he was leaving a year early to enter the 1998 NFL Draft. Peyton Manning of Tennessee was already considered the top quarterback heading into the draft. With Leaf's declaration, it became a daily debate by the media and football fans about which quarterback was better. NFL teams in need of a quarterback were split on which signal-caller promised long-term success. When Leaf arrived for the NFL Combine in February, he was found to be twenty pounds heavier than he was just six weeks prior. That raised a red flag for a number of teams.

Not long after, the Indianapolis Colts, who were picking first, set up meetings with both quarterbacks to get a better feel for who they preferred. Indy had a great meeting with Manning. On the day of Leaf's meeting with the team, he failed to show. Out in California, the San Diego Chargers also needed a quarterback and traded up with the Arizona Cardinals for the second overall selection.

On the day of the draft, Indianapolis chose Manning first and San Diego took Leaf second. That transaction meant that, in fewer than twenty years, WSU's program had four quarterbacks selected in the first round of the NFL Draft: Jack Thompson, Timm Rosenbach (in the supplemental draft), Drew Bledsoe and now Leaf. Leon Bender was selected in the second round by the Oakland Raiders, Dorian Boose was picked in the same round by the New York Jets and Jason McEndoo was selected in the seventh round by the Seattle Seahawks. Sadly, Bender passd away suddenly just weeks after the draft due to complications from epilepsy.

Leaf began the 1998 season as San Diego's starting quarterback, but poor play and a poor attitude limited him to nine starts. After the second game of the year, Leaf was caught on video yelling at a newspaper reporter and had to be restrained by teammates. His rookie season ended with 1,289 yards, 2 touchdowns and 15 interceptions. In 1999, a serious shoulder injury put Leaf on injured reserve, and he missed the entire season. A year later, he returned to the starter's role and passed for 1,883 yards, 11 touchdowns and 18 picks. The Chargers went 1-15, and Leaf was released in early 2001. During his time in San Diego, Leaf won four of his eighteen starts. He was then on the roster of the Tampa Bay Buccaneers and Dallas Cowboys for short stints. He was out of football by the fall of 2002. Leaf's brief pro career ended with 3,666 total passing yards, 14 touchdowns and 36 interceptions. Years later, he would admit that leaving college early was a mistake, not only because of the friends and coaches he left behind but also because of his NFL experiences.

9

JASON GESSER RAISES THE BAR

Saint Louis School in Honolulu, Hawaii, is known for producing good quarterbacks. Since the mid-1990s alone, names such as Darnell Arceneaux, Timmy Chang, Marcus Mariota and Tua Tagovailoa have led the Fighting Crusaders. Wedged between Arceneaux and Chang's years of service was Jason Gesser, who starred for Saint Louis in 1996 and 1997. As a junior in '96, Gesser led the Crusaders to a state championship and was selected to the all-state team. The following season, Saint Louis repeated as state champions, while Gesser became a PrepStar All-West selection as well as an Academic All-American. In Gesser's two years as a starter, the Crusaders had an impressive 24-0 record. Gesser's high school stats brought the attention of several high-profile colleges, including Washington State.

At the same time that Gesser was piling up awards in Hawaii, the Cougars and Ryan Leaf were making their run to the 1997 Rose Bowl. That fall, Mike Price also spent considerable time looking for his next quarterback. He loved the intangibles that Gesser brought to the table and did what he could to bring the Honolulu quarterback to Pullman. NCAA rules at the time stipulated that Coach Price could make only one home visit to a recruit, and Price visited the Gesser home early in the year. After his visit, Price's son Eric, a WSU assistant coach, began spending a lot of time with the Gesser family.

"The Gessers really liked Eric's personality, and he became fast friends with the family. Eric pretty much lived with them and got to know Jason's dad and his grandparents as well," commented Mike Price in 2022.

After months of deliberating, Gesser narrowed his choices to WSU, Washington and Oregon. Ultimately, Gesser found himself gravitating toward the Palouse.

"Jason fell in love with the small school atmosphere and the coaches at WSU, and that's what helped us bring him here," continued Price. "I still had fun with him after he got here, though, especially with the weather and Jason coming from Hawaii. We'd be on the ground stretching before practice during the snowy, cold winter months, then I look at him and I say, 'Why did you come here?' And he'd say, 'Because of you. You were the one that talked me into it!'"

Gesser redshirted in 1998 and then received some playing time in 1999 that amounted to 445 yards passing and 3 interceptions. Despite being just a sophomore and having barely played, the team voted Gesser its captain before the 2000 season. His teammates didn't look at his previous year's stats. They saw Gesser's leadership every day in practice and his ability to bond with everyone on the field. "Jason was a great leader, and a great person, and so well liked," recalled Price. "Being a captain when you're a sophomore, with a losing football team, it doesn't happen very often."

Gesser was on the gridiron for nine games in 2000 and couldn't do much to prevent a 3-2 start from sliding to a 4-7 finish for the Cougars (three of the losses were in overtime). As he picked up on the intricacies of Price's offense, Gesser's play improved from 1999, as he passed for 1,967 yards, 16 touchdowns and 10 interceptions.

At the dawn of the 2001 season, Gesser's teammates once again voted him team captain. The '01 Cougars were a mix of veteran talent and a lot of Gesser moxie. WSU's defense alone had no less than four defensive backs who became NFL players after leaving Pullman. They included Marcus Trufant, Jason David, Lamont Thompson and Erik Coleman. (David won Super Bowl XLI as a member of the Indianapolis Colts.)

The Cougs burst out of the gate in 2001 with seven straight victories before losing to eleventh-ranked Oregon on October 27. Two victories followed before the Washington Huskies defeated their cross-state rivals in the Apple Cup. WSU's 9-2 record got them an invite to the Sun Bowl, where they played the Purdue Boilermakers. Purdue held a 20–17 lead at halftime, but the Cougs pulled away for a 33–27 victory. The bowl win was Price's third as WSU's head coach, once again eclipsing any coach in program history. He also owned two ten-win seasons after the Sun Bowl put WSU's final record at 10-2. Then, for the second time in his WSU tenure, Price was named Pac-10 Coach of the Year. Gesser came into his own during the season and put himself on the map as one of the nation's best quarterbacks. In 2001, he passed for 3,010 yards (first in the Pac-10), 26 touchdowns and 13 interceptions and added 101 rushing yards with 2 rushing scores.

"God, Jason scrambled like crazy and made throws and was just an unbelievable fighter, competitor. Always had a chance to win when he was in the game," remarked Price in 2022. At that point, Gesser ranked fifth in WSU history in passing yards and total offense. But, as good as his '01 season was, Gesser would only get better in 2002.

Optimism surrounding WSU in 2002 was sky-high. In addition to Gesser, now a senior, the Cougs returned Coleman, Trufant and David in the secondary. Receiver Devard Darling arrived that year after transferring from Florida State, where his twin brother, Devaughan, died during a Seminoles practice. Mike Bush further bolstered the receiving core, hoping to add to his 46 catches and 10 touchdowns from the previous season. Rounding out the offense was receiver Jerome Riley and running backs Jermaine Green and John Tippins. Gesser was voted team captain before the season, making him the only Cougar in program history to be selected captain three consecutive years.

The 2002 season began with a bang when WSU crushed the Nevada Wolfpack, 31–7, in Seattle for the Cougar Gridiron Classic. That win was followed by a 49–14 thumping of Idaho. In mid-September, WSU headed to Columbus to face Ohio State. The Buckeyes were ranked sixth in the nation, and the Cougars were ranked tenth. What should have been a competitive game was anything but, as over 104,000 fans witnessed Ohio State defeat WSU, 25–7. One week later, the Cougs got back on track after waxing Montana State, 45–28. Then, while nursing a dislocated rib, Gesser threw 44 passes in a 48–38 win over Cal on September 28. Next up was Pete Carroll and his eighteenth-ranked USC team, a must-have game that prompted Tippins to make a speech to his teammates the night before the game. "I had the senior speech last night and I told the team, 'This game right here is going to make or break us,'" said Tippins. "'This puts us on the map. This shows people we're a great team.'"

The matchup was a battle between Gesser and the Trojans' Carson Palmer, resulting in a plethora of NFL scouts on hand to witness which signal-caller was more pro-ready. As expected, the two teams were coached well and rarely gave ground. In fact, the Cougars' defense held the USC ground game to just 72 total yards. By halftime, the score was 10–7 in favor of Washington State. In the second half, the teams traded scores before the fourth quarter ended in a 27-all tie. With the entire congregation of Martin

Jason Gesser in action. *WSU Athletics*.

Stadium on their feet in overtime, the home crowd roared with delight when Cougs' defensive tackle Rien Long sacked Palmer twice.

"Bringing the heat, that's our motto," said Cougs defender Isaac Brown. "Just keep on bringing the heat."

With both teams sucking oxygen, WSU kicker Drew Dunning became the hero of the day when he booted a 35-yard field goal to win the contest. Displaying the ice in his veins, Dunning had previously nailed another 35-yarder to send the game into overtime. Once the winning kick proved true, he was immediately carried off the field by the Cougar faithful. "Four students picked me up and carried me off the field," Dunning said. "They almost dropped me."

Palmer and Gesser did their part to make things interesting. Gesser threw 44 passes for 315 yards, 2 touchdowns and 1 pick. Palmer tossed 50 passes for 381 yards, 2 passing scores and 1 interception. Gesser did a stand-up job in getting his fellow offensive mates involved. Tippins and Green rushed for 79 and 92 yards, respectively, and four Cougar receivers had more than 50 receiving yards.

"I didn't think there was any way we were going to get 500 yards of offense on this team," said Price. "If we can beat this team, we're for real."

In the confines of the team locker room, Gesser handed the game ball to Price and explained to a writer how much the coach meant to him and the team. "This guy has done so much for us and for Cougar football," Gesser said. "He's the longest reigning coach in the Pac-10 and he finally got his win against USC up here in Martin Stadium. I'm proud to be writing history with him," Gesser continued. "Hopefully we'll keep writing history together."

WSU's big win over USC propelled them through the rest of October, when they defeated Stanford and Arizona. When the calendar turned to November, the Cougs bullied sixteenth-ranked Arizona State, 44–22, on November 2 and then faced fifteenth-ranked Oregon at home on November 9. The Ducks had become a very good football team under Mike Bellotti, Ryan Leaf's former nemesis. In 2000, Oregon lost only two games. Then, in 2001, the team ranked second in the country with an 11-1 record and a win over Colorado in the Fiesta Bowl. One of the Ducks' victories in '01 was a 24–17 defeat of WSU. In 2000, Bellotti's team ended Gesser's season when his leg was broken on a sack. It was high time that Price and Gesser reversed WSU's fortunes against the Ducks in 2002.

"We are going to be so focused for this game," said Price a week before the Oregon game. "Everything we are going to do is to play the best we can for this Saturday."

"We want this game real bad," added Gesser.

The problem with hype, especially in sports, is that it rarely lives up to itself. Oregon's team in 2002 was not even close to the squad they were in 2001. On their way to an eventual 7-6 record, the Ducks lost to Gesser and the Cougs, 32–21. It wasn't without some mistakes by Gesser. He had the ball stripped from him and returned for a score in the first quarter and then threw a pick-six in the third quarter. Price comically pointed out the blunders to reporters after the game.

"Jason, I think he was actually going for the Heisman Trophy through Oregon and Washington State," Price said. "He was trying to get some Oregon voters to vote for him. He was involved in six touchdowns, two for Oregon and four for us. That was a little unusual way to try and get the voters from Oregon, but it might work."

WSU's victory moved the team to third in the country heading into their Apple Cup game against Washington. The Huskies were 6-5, but there was extra incentive for them to keep Washington State from a second Rose Bowl appearance in six years.

"Husky and Cougar fans gotta love this," said Price after the Oregon game. "We're playing for the Pac-10 championship and for the Rose Bowl and you're playing your cross-state opponent. That's the way I'd like it to be every Apple Cup and I know Rick (Neuheisel) would too. A chance for them to knock us off and a chance for us to secure the Rose Bowl bid. It's a perfect situation to be in."

PRESSURE? WHAT PRESSURE? GOING back to his redshirt year in 1998, Jason Gesser and the Cougars had lost to Washington in the Apple Cup each season. One of the team's two losses in 2001 was to the Huskies, and that loss had prevented an invitation to a major bowl. In 2002, Washington State had only one loss and was undefeated in conference play, and only two teams were ranked higher than them in the nation. Before the '02 Apple Cup, the press made sure to mention that Gesser was the winningest quarterback in WSU history. He was 19-3 in two years, which was the third-best mark by a quarterback in the NCAA at that point. It didn't seem logical. The program has produced Jack Thompson, Mark Rypien, Timm Rosenbach, Drew Bledsoe and Ryan Leaf. Yet, Jason Gesser, in terms of wins, was better than his predecessors. In fact, Gesser was on his way to 3,408 passing yards in 2002. That gave him two consecutive years with over 3,000 yards passing. None of the Cougar greats who came before him had accomplished such a feat. Only Leaf's 3,968 passing yards in 1997 was better than Gesser's 2002 yardage.

One might have thought that Gesser was paralyzed from the intensity of the moment as the Cougs got set to face the Huskies. Yet, on the day of the game, an article in the Spokane *Spokesman-Review* profiled Gesser's love of ketchup, flip-flops and surfing. If he was nervous, Gesser wasn't letting it show. Not even a showdown with the Huskies' Cody Pickett (3,818 passing yards) made Gesser flinch.

After the ninety-fifth Apple Cup got underway, Washington was the first to score. Pickett called his own number on a 1-yard quarterback sneak with 8:54 remaining in the first quarter. With 4:00 left in the quarter, WSU's Dunning kicked a 34-yard field goal to cut Washington's lead to 7–3. In the second quarter, Jermaine Green scored from 2 yards out, and a 67-yard bomb from Gesser to receiver Sammy Moore put the Cougars up, 17–7. The top offense in the Pac-10 had just scored 17 unanswered points on their biggest rival.

The third quarter produced only a field goal from Washington's John Anderson. The score was still 17–10 in the fourth quarter when Gesser was knocked from the game with a high ankle sprain on a sack by the Huskies' Tank Johnson. "The way he pulled me down, my leg got folded back and it was awkward and I heard a bunch of popping in my ankle and knee, and that was it," Gesser reminisced in 2012.

WSU would increase their lead to 20–10 on a Dunning kick with 4:44 remaining. Washington clawed back with a 7-yard touchdown pass from Pickett to Paul Arnold with 3:29 remaining to cut the Cougar lead to 20–17. Then, with Gesser watching helplessly on the sideline, Anderson tied the game with a 20-yard field goal just before the final whistle. With the score knotted at 20-all, the contest went into overtime. Both squads kicked a field goal to tie the game at 23 and send it into double overtime. In the second overtime, Anderson and Dunning kicked two more field goals to keep the score tied at 26 and send the game into a third overtime, unprecedented for the Apple Cup.

Anderson connected on a 49-yard kick in the third overtime to give the Huskies the lead, 29–26. Gesser's replacement, Matt Kegel, and the WSU offense took over on the next possession and looked to get the ball into the end zone. Instead, on the very first play of the drive, Kegel dropped back and attempted a pass, only for the ball to be tipped and knocked to the ground by Washington's Kai Ellis. It looked initially like the referee signaled for an incompletion, which would have set up second down for the Cougs.

After a brief huddle, head referee Gordon Riese clicked on his microphone to tell the crowd and television audience the ruling on the field. "The ruling on the field was that it was a backward pass. Washington recovered that pass, and the game is over," Riese announced.

As the Huskies sprinted off the field in jubilant celebration after their improbable 29–26 win, the Cougars were stunned. The play was examined numerous times by the media, and it was unclear in which direction the ball was actually traveling when Kegel released it. For Husky players and fans, the ball definitely went backward. As expected, the Cougars claimed that the ball was going forward and that Ellis's tip knocked the pass off target. Therefore, the play should have been ruled an incomplete pass and WSU given a second down. "That's wrong," Price told a referee as he walked off the field. "That was just a bad pass. It was a forward pass," he said.

"It was a shame the game was decided on a questionable call," assistant coach Bill Doba said. "Of course, we thought it was a forward pass, and they thought it was a backward pass. It would have been nice to see the game finished on the field. I guess in Washington's view, it was."

Price was still upset with the call when he was interviewed about the game on the ten-year anniversary in 2012. "BS call," he said. "I mean, c'mon, to make a call like that to make a difference in the game like that?"

Players and coaches from both sides dodged a cascade of bottles thrown by the Martin Stadium faithful as they made their way to their respective locker rooms. Once he retreated to safety, Gesser was asked if he believed there would have been a different outcome had he not been injured. "It's not the way you want to finish up your career," said Gesser, a senior. "I don't get hurt, we would have won that game."

THANKFULLY, THE DISAPPOINTING END to the Apple Cup didn't mean the end for the Cougars. They still had a game against UCLA on December 7. If they won that game, WSU would have a share of the Pac-10 title (with USC) and still be eligible for the Rose Bowl. There was some talk that Gesser would be unavailable for the game due to his injuries and that Kegel would have to take his place. Thankfully, there was a two-week break between the Washington and UCLA games, and Gesser wasn't about to leave destiny in the hands of someone else. He started the contest and was practically duct-taped together, complete with braces on his right knee and ankle and a flak vest protecting his sore ribs. The Bruins made a game of it at first, but by halftime, Gesser and his crew were running away with it. WSU's defense gave up only 6 points in the second half, and Washington State had its second consecutive ten-win season after an emphatic 48–27 win.

"I'm feeling no pain right now," Gesser said after the game while photographers snapped pictures of him with a rose in his mouth. "Just because my leg hurts now, I wasn't going to let my dream pass me by," he continued.

"He is the toughest guy in college football. As bad as he was limping, it's unbelievable what he did. Washington State is lucky to have a leader like him," UCLA cornerback Ricky Manning said.

Gesser's 24-10 record as a starter was the best in program history. The Cougars won ten games in back-to-back years, which was a first in team history. Best of all, the team was headed to the Rose Bowl for the second time in five years, also unprecedented in WSU history.

"To go to the Rose Bowl two times in five years is really something for our program, for our players, our coaches, and really for our school," Price said. "I would never say I couldn't expect Jason to do something, because that's the kind of guy he is. He's got to be the MVP of Washington State history."

The Cougar team did honor Gesser as their team MVP for 2002. With the regular season now behind them, awards season began. Gesser was named Pac-10 Co-Offensive Player of the Year with USC's Palmer, and he finished seventh in the Heisman Trophy balloting (Palmer won the award). Additionally, he was named an All-American and earned his fourth Academic All-Pac-10 award.

DUE TO THEIR WIN against the Bruins, WSU was ranked seventh in the country. Their opponent would be eighth-ranked Oklahoma, who was entering their first-ever Rose Bowl with just two losses of their own. Nate Hybl was the Sooners' starting quarterback. The Oklahoma defense featured corner Andre Woolfolk, who would be a first-round pick in the 2003 NFL Draft, and defensive tackle Tommie Harris, who had been the *Sports Illustrated* cover boy for that magazine's 2002 preseason college football issue.

Washington State prepared for the Rose Bowl with heavy hearts. Just two weeks before the game, Price agonized before accepting the head coach position at storied University of Alabama. He had given fourteen years to the Cougars and was easily the most successful head coach in school history. It was now time to give the SEC a try. Dennis Erickson had proven that his offense could work at the highest levels of college football, and now Price was taking his turn. After announcing his decision on December 18,

Jason Gesser during the 2003 Rose Bowl. *WSU Athletics.*

Price explained why he was leaving. "I just can't pass it up," Price said. "I'm getting up there. I've got to do this for my family."

The Alabama job was a huge bump in pay for Price. In 2002, he had made $900,000 with incentives. His new contract with the Crimson Tide would pay the coach $14 million over seven years.

"You can't help but be upset," said WSU defensive tackle Jeremey Williams. "We thought he would be here forever, but that's the way it goes. We just have to go win the Rose Bowl now."

Whether it was the aura of Price leaving or the fact that the Sooners were a much better team, Washington State got their tails handed to them. The Cougars kept Oklahoma honest by allowing just 3 points in the first quarter.

After that, it was all Sooners. Hybl and the Oklahoma special teams unit ran away with it and scored 27 points before WSU scored their first. The final outcome was a sad, disappointing 34–14 loss for WSU.

"I think aliens came and took our team away," said a dejected Cougars fan after the game.

Gesser was beside himself for not sending Price (who coached WSU during the game) out a winner. "I didn't want to send him out that way," Gesser said. "A lot of guys didn't want to send him out that way, but football's football."

Price hugged his players after the game, and a few tears rolled down his cheeks, fully realizing he was leaving the place he had called home after so long. "I have given twenty years of my life [including time as an assistant] to Washington State, and I think the university is better off for what I have accomplished," Price said.

THE CONCLUSION OF THE Rose Bowl signified the conclusion of Jason Gesser's collegiate career. He arrived in Pullman as a standout quarterback from Hawaii and exited WSU as arguably its all-time best signal-caller. When he graduated, Gesser owned team marks in career starts (34), total yards (9,007), pass attempts (1,118), completions (611), touchdown passes (70) and consecutive games with a touchdown pass (25). He was also the only Washington State quarterback to play in two bowl games. Despite all his records, Gesser was not selected in the 2003 NFL Draft and was instead signed as a free agent by the Tennessee Titans. He was buried on the Titans' depth chart and released by the organization before the 2004 season. In 2005, Gesser found work in Canada, where he started two games for the Calgary Stampeders. Both games were victories, and Gesser passed for 356 yards, 4 touchdowns and 5 interceptions before sustaining an ankle injury. Calgary released Gesser after '05, and he was signed by the Utah Blaze of the Arena Football League in 2006. In two seasons with the Blaze, Gesser passed for over 1,000 yards, 24 touchdowns and 7 interceptions.

When the 2007 AFL season ended, Gesser never played another down of football. He got into coaching and was employed at the high school and college levels, including stops at Idaho and Wyoming. While at Idaho in 2012, Gesser was named interim coach when head coach Robb Akey was fired after eight games. Unfortunately, Gesser could not coax any wins out of his Vandals and ended the season with four losses. Idaho did not retain Gesser after 2012, and he became the quarterbacks coach at Wyoming in 2013. After one season with the Cowboys, Gesser returned to WSU to work in the school's athletic office.

MIKE LEACH RESTORES
THE COUGARS

When Mike Price left Washington State for Alabama after the 2002 season, he was replaced by Bill Doba.

Doba had been a member of the WSU coaching staff since Price arrived in 1989. Between 1994 and 2002, Doba was the associate head coach, defensive coordinator and linebackers coach for the Cougars. With Price now gone, it seemed only natural for Doba to be elevated. In 2003, quarterback Matt Kegel passed for 2,947 yards and 21 touchdowns as WSU finished with their third consecutive ten-win season. The year was highlighted by the play of receiver Devard Darling, who had 50 receptions for 830 yards, and running back Jonathan Smith, who paced the ground attack with 961 rushing yards. The second week of the season saw a near-titanic upset when the Cougs came up short against nineteenth-ranked Notre Dame in overtime, 29–26. In the Holiday Bowl against fifth-ranked University of Texas, WSU (ranked fifteenth in the nation) upset the Longhorns, 28–20.

Unfortunately, the good times for Washington State and Coach Doba ended after that glorious season. The next four years were dismal, as the Cougs could do no better than six wins. When the 2007 season concluded, Doba was fired and Washington State hired former Cougar Paul Wulff. During his collegiate playing career, Wulff had the opportunity to suit up with Timm Rosenbach and play for both Dennis Erickson and Mike Price. Before arriving in Pullman to replace Doba, Wulff had been the head coach at Eastern Washington University. There he compiled a 53-40 record that included two Big Sky Conference co-championships and three

Big Sky Conference Coach of the Year awards. During his introductory press conference at WSU, Wulff made a bold shot across the bow to the Washington Huskies. "Dogs hunt and bark, but Cougars fight and kill," said Wulff.

Those attending the second game of Wulff's tenure watched the Cal Bears tattoo Washington State by 63, the worst defeat in team history. Many more lopsided losses would follow in 2008. In four years as the coach of the Cougs, Wulff had a 9-40 record and was fired after the 2011 season.

Weary of eight straight years of losing football, WSU athletic director Bill Moos went looking for a coach who could turn things around. Moos had left WSU in 1990 and led athletics at the University of Montana and the University of Oregon before returning to Pullman in 2010. One of his first orders of business was to restore the Cougar football program. Moos had a very short list of who he was interested in and looked outside the Cougar program for help. In mid-November 2011, he made his way to the southern tip of Florida and sought an audience with former Texas Tech head coach Mike Leach.

"I felt if we had a chance to get Mike Leach, I had to set the foundation before the season was over. To tell you the truth, he was the only guy I talked to and the only guy I wanted," said Moos in 2011.

During his decade with Tech, Leach had used his love of the aerial game to consistently put the Red Raiders on the map. Beginning with his first season in Lubbock, in 2000, Leach guided Texas Tech to bowl appearances every year. Additionally, the program never had fewer than seven wins. They won eleven games in 2008, when the team was ranked as high as second in the country and featured quarterback Graham Harrell and receiver Michael Crabtree. One year later, Leach passed Spike Dykes as the winningest football coach in school history.

Near the end of the 2009 season, Leach was questioned by Texas Tech administrators over his treatment of Red Raiders running back Adam James. James had received a concussion during a December practice for the upcoming Alamo Bowl and was told not to practice the following day by team doctors. James later claimed that Leach ordered him to stay in a darkened equipment room rather than attend practice. To make matters worse, James is the son of former SMU great Craig James, who also spent time as a talking head with ESPN. When Adam James told his father about the banishment to the equipment room, Craig became angry. He contacted Tech administrators and demanded answers. After Leach was summoned to tell his side of the story, he was ordered to write an apology to Adam James or face suspension. Leach's attorney countered by describing an alternative explanation for the incident and that James had been treated appropriately. When Leach failed to produce a written apology, Texas Tech fired him on December 30. Barely a week later, Leach sued the school for wrongful termination along with several other claims. Eventually, both a district court and the Texas Supreme Court dismissed all of Leach's claims. During the two years that followed, Leach spent time as an analyst for CBS and SiriusXM. He also wrote and published a book, *Swing Your Sword: Leading the Charge in Football and in Life*. Not long after, Moos caught up with Leach and offered him the job at Washington State, and Leach accepted.

Leach, who passed away suddenly in December 2022, had always been something of a character who did his own thing and pursued his many interests whenever he could. He loved pirate history and could regale visitors about any aspect of pirating. Originally, Leach had pursued a law degree and obtained his juris doctorate from Pepperdine University in 1986. But he had a fascination with football and coaching that he couldn't get out of his head.

"I wanted to coach at a young age. I had posters on my wall growing up of Bart Starr, Johnny Unitas, those types of guys," said Leach in early 2022. "I was already thinking about coaching when I was playing baseball as a youth."

The itch to coach football proved too great. He attended BYU as an undergrad and was enthralled with the passing attack of head coach Lavell Edwards and quarterback Steve Young. Even after leaving BYU to attend Pepperdine, Leach was mesmerized by offensive football. That's when he made a decision that would shape the rest of his life. "I decided I was going to coach for one to three years, then go back to the law if I needed to," said Leach in 2022.

Leaving the law behind, Leach began his career as a lowly graduate assistant before latching on with Cal Poly as an offensive line coach. After a brief stop in Finland to coach the sport, Leach made his way to Iowa Wesleyan in Mount Pleasant, Iowa, in 1989. It was there that he began to hone his own passing attack alongside Hal Mumme, a fellow aficionado of the forward pass. The two were like mad scientists in a lab, developing the "Air Raid" offense and spending the 1990s deploying their creation at such stops as Valdosta State and the University of Kentucky. As they perfected their offense, Leach and Mumme couldn't help but keep an eye on Washington State, where Erickson and Price were defying the run-first mentality of many college coaches. Their one-back offense only served to show Leach and Mumme that they were on the right track.

"I really liked WSU's history with their offense and especially their quarterbacks," Leach commented in 2022. "Dennis and Mike already proved you could throw the football with success."

In 1999, Leach was hired as the offensive coordinator and quarterbacks coach at Oklahoma before getting hired by Texas Tech in 2000. His time in Lubbock only cemented Leach's status as a coach who loved to throw the pigskin. At one point, Tech led the entire NCAA in passing yardage for four straight years. So his banishment from the game in 2010 and 2011 didn't dampen Leach's enthusiasm for the game. If anything, his exile made him want to prove himself more to the doubters. That desire would be a huge benefit for Washington State.

"We've got a coach that, I believe, his peers in this conference are going to take notice. and we are on our way, in my opinion, to a great future with Cougar football," said Moos after hiring Leach for $2.25 million per year.

The 2012 Cougars had two quarterbacks on the roster, senior Jeff Tuel and rising sophomore Connor Halliday, whom Leach inherited. Unfortunately, Leach also inherited a locker room full of headaches. Under Doba and Wulff, the Cougars were in the news for all the wrong reasons. In 2008, the media reported that there had been an astounding twenty-five arrests of WSU players in the previous year and a half. Furthermore, the Cougs weren't applying themselves in the classroom. The NCAA took away eight scholarships tied to that organization's Academic Progress Rate standards. The loose-cannon attitude had persisted, and Leach wasn't happy. His first season was spent installing both his high-octane offense and some much-needed team discipline. As WSU limped through a 3-8 season (which included an overtime Apple Cup victory), as many as eighteen Cougars were kicked off the team or quit on their own. Leach couldn't contain his displeasure on a number of occasions, banning his athletes from Twitter and lambasting his seniors.

"Some of them have this zombie-like, go-through-the-motions, that's how-its-always-been, that's-how-it-will-always-be, empty-corpse quality," Leach explained during his weekly press conference halfway through the '12 season.

Weeks after his zombie comment, Leach had something to say about his receivers regarding their lack of effort. "All of a sudden, our fragile little receivers are going to go into the end zone and get frightened. So they can't catch the ball. That's crazy. They just need to learn to be tougher," said an exasperated Leach.

If the Cougar players didn't like Leach's criticism, Moos and many of the locals appreciated what he was trying to do. "I think this change is long overdue," Moos said. "We got a real task. Mike doesn't waver. He is not wishy-washy."

"I treat my constituency far better," said WSU professor and Pullman mayor Glenn Johnson. "They are not the walking dead. But, there are two camps right now," he continued. "From my standpoint, he's trying to change the culture and build a program."

After clearing out the riffraff, the Cougars improved to 6-7 in 2013, which included a high-scoring 48–45 loss to Colorado State in the New Mexico Bowl. Like Dennis Erickson years before him, Leach had WSU in a bowl game in just his second season. The program cratered to three wins in 2014 before the Air Raid offense got nine wins and a 20–14 victory over the Miami Hurricanes in the 2015 Sun Bowl. In 2016 and 2017, WSU won eight and nine games, respectively, before losing in the Holiday Bowl both seasons. That marked the first time in school history that a coach took the Cougars to three consecutive bowl games and four in a five-year stretch. Between the 2015 and 2017 seasons, quarterback Luke Falk, a former walk-on, turned opposing secondaries into Swiss cheese. In '15 and '16, he passed for over

Coach Mike Leach holding up the 2015 Sun Bowl Trophy after WSU defeated the Miami Hurricanes. *WSU Athletics.*

Mike Leach on the sidelines during a game against the University of Oregon in 2016. *WSU Athletics*.

Mike Leach running onto the field before a 2015 game against the University of Wyoming. *WSU Athletics*.

4,000 yards and still holds several conference records. When Falk left WSU for the NFL after the 2017 season, Leach went looking for another record-setting quarterback to replace him.

IT JUST SO HAPPENED that Gardner Minshew was looking for a new home in 2018. He had grown up in Mississippi and developed a love for football as a youth. When he was in middle school, Minshew's father, Flint, used Leach's Air Raid offense for Gardner's flag football team. Minshew then became quarterback for the Brandon (Mississippi) High School Bulldogs and led the team to the state championship game as a sophomore. The Bulldogs lost that day, but they returned two years later and won the title game. During his prep career, Minshew passed for 9,705 yards, 88 touchdowns and 24 interceptions and rushed for over 1,400 yards and 17 more touchdowns. He committed to play at Troy University but left before playing a down. Minshew then made his way to Northwest Mississippi Junior College, where he battered the competition during the 2015 season and helped the Rangers to an NJCAA national title. The following year, Minshew enrolled at East Carolina University and played for the Pirates in 2016 and 2017. In 2017, Minshew passed for 2,140 yards and 16 touchdowns and then graduated with a degree in communications.

Despite graduating, Minshew still had a year of playing eligibility left. He put out feelers and received interest from Nick Saban and the University of Alabama. Minshew posted this news to gauge possible interest from other schools, as he believed he wouldn't actually start for the Tide. At approximately the same time, WSU quarterback Tyler Hilinski tragically committed suicide, leaving the program and Pullman community in mourning. With Hilinski's passing, the Cougars needed another veteran quarterback. That's when Leach made his sales pitch to Minshew.

"I asked Gardner, 'Do you want to hold a clipboard at Alabama or lead the nation in passing?'" recalled Leach in 2022. "It didn't take long to convince him."

IT WASN'T LIKE MINSHEW was automatically the starter after signing with WSU. He still had to compete against Anthony Gordon and Trey Tinsley during spring ball. That turned out to be a formality, as Minshew worked his way to the top of the depth chart by the time the 2018 season began. Leach was as good as his promise to Minshew. After the first six games

Left: Gardner Minshew versus Cal. *WSU Athletics*.

Below: Gardner Minshew versus Utah. *WSU Athletics*.

Coach Mike Leach (*center*) and quarterback Gardner Minshew (*left*) celebrate WSU's victory over Iowa State in the 2018 Alamo Bowl. *WSU Athletics.*

of the season, Minshew led the NCAA in passing yards (2,422), attempts (313) and completions (215). In a game against the Arizona Wildcats in November, Minshew set a single-game program record with 7 touchdowns in a 69–28 thumping.

By then, it was Minshew mania across the country. WSU's prolific offense ranked fifteenth in the country in points per game, and Minshew (who resembled a 1970s beat cop with his dark, horseshoe mustache) was slinging footballs at a record rate. Entering the 111th Apple Cup game, WSU was ranked eighth in the nation with a 10-1 record, then lost to Washington for the sixth straight year. The Cougs met the Iowa State Cyclones in the Alamo Bowl, and Minshew passed for 299 yards and 2 touchdowns and rushed for another to win, 28–26. During the contest, Minshew completed 35 passes, which set an Alamo Bowl record.

With his final year behind him, Minshew could bask in the glory of what he had accomplished. Remarkably, he supplanted Halliday for WSU's single-season passing record (4,597 yards in 2013) with 4,776 passing yards along with his 38 touchdowns and 9 interceptions. Minshew also broke the Pac-12 single-season passing yardage mark set by former Cal quarterback Jared Goff. The accolades continued, as he was named first-team All-Pac-12 and the Offensive Player of the Year for the conference. Minshew received the Johnny Unitas Golden Arm Award and finished fifth in the Heisman Trophy balloting. In the 2019 NFL Draft, the Jacksonville Jaguars selected Minshew as the 178th overall pick in the sixth round. He then became a member of the Philadelphia Eagles in 2021. He was signed by the Indianapolis Colts on March 17, 2023.

WITH MINSHEW GONE TO the NFL, Washington State took a step backward in 2019 and finished 6-7, including a 31–21 loss to Air Force in the Cheeze-It Bowl. On January 9, 2020, Leach made a move to the SEC when he signed a contract to coach the Mississippi State Bulldogs. During his eight years in Pullman, Leach had a 55-47 overall record and took the program to an unprecedented six bowl games, including a bowl in five straight seasons. He is third on the all-time WSU wins list behind Babe Hollingbery (93) and Mike Price (83). When he arrived at the school in 2012, Leach acknowledged both Erickson and Price for what they did to put Cougar football on the map.

"We're going to try to do everything here," Leach said during his press conference. "Win as much as we can at the highest level we can attain. What Mike Price did here [two Rose Bowls] will stand the test of time. There's

Mike Leach on the sideline during a game against the University of Northern Colorado in 2019. *WSU Athletics.*

a tradition. I've watched Dennis's teams, gained inspiration from him, attended his practices, drawn on what he's done, and my suspicion is that what we do is congruent with what he had in mind all along."

As a neophyte offensive coach in the early 1980s, Leach took the information that he gleaned from Erickson and Price and mixed in some of his own strategies. It's fitting that the "student" eventually brought a potent passing attack to the school where the "teachers" had made passing fashionable. Leach helped restore a program that had fallen on hard times and then handed it off to the next generation of young coaches. It would be their turn to continue the legacy of those who came before them.

EPILOGUE

In this section, we'll catch up with a few of the people highlighted in this book.

Dennis Erickson

When Ryan Leaf visited Dennis Erickson at the University of Miami in the fall of 1993, Erickson told the quarterback he had designs on leaving for the Seattle Seahawks if the situation presented itself. It turns out that he must have doubled as a seer, because the situation did present itself in 1995. The Seahawks fired Tom Flores after the 1994 season and brought Erickson home to the Pacific Northwest for roughly $1 million per year. He spent four years in Seattle, where he coached WSU alum Broussard as well as John Friesz, his quarterback from Idaho. Erickson put together a 31-33 record and was fired after the 1998 season. Next was a return to the college ranks and a four-year run at Oregon State, followed by two years as the head coach of the San Francisco 49ers. During his second year with the 49ers, in 2004, Erickson's father, "Pinky," passed away at the age of seventy-nine. In 2006, Idaho brought Erickson back to where his college head coaching career began. That lasted for a season before Erickson left to guide Arizona State from 2007 through the 2011 season. He then spent 2013–16 at the University of Utah as an assistant before his brief stint with the Salt Lake Stallions of the Alliance of American Football. Erickson currently resides in the Coeur d'Alene, Idaho area. He is a member of the College Football Hall of Fame.

TIMM ROSENBACH

Timm Rosenbach's 1989 rookie year in the NFL was rather uneventful. Cardinals head coach Gene Stallings was fired partway through the season, and Joe Bugel took over the team in 1990. Bugel installed Rosenbach as the starter in 1990, and the WSU alum started all sixteen games and passed for 3,098 yards, 16 touchdowns and 17 interceptions. He also ran the ball 86 times for 470 yards and 3 touchdowns while the Cardinals won five games for the second year in a row. Rosenbach struggled with injuries in 1991 and began to have doubts about continuing to play such a violent sport. That was made even more clear when former WSU teammate Mike Utley was permanently injured the same season. After blocking for Rosenbach as a Cougar, Utley had been drafted by the Detroit Lions in 1989 and worked his way to the starter's spot at right guard in '91. In Week 12 against the Los Angeles Rams, Utley severely injured his spinal cord and was permanently paralyzed from the chest down. As he was carted off the field, Utley raised his hand and gave the Lions crowd a thumbs-up. The image was played nationally as Utley's injury made headlines. Watching at home, Rosenbach was devastated at the sight of his friend and former protector. "I can tell you what was going through my mind," recalled Rosenbach in 2022. "I was like, 'Why do we play this game?' That's always going through my mind. I was like, 'Why am I doing this? That's my guy.'"

In 1992, Rosenbach started three games and was injured again. At that point, the idea of playing sixteen games in the NFL had lost its luster.

"I thought I was turning into some kind of animal," Rosenbach told the *New York Times* in 1993. "You go through a week getting yourself up for a game by hating the other team, the other players. You're so mean and hateful, you want to kill somebody. Football's so aggressive. Things get done by force. And then you come home, you're supposed to turn it off? I had become a machine. I became sick of it."

It didn't help that the defensive players in the pros were built like Mac trucks and could hit with similar force.

"Reggie White, he is very religious, and he'd hit you a murderous shot and then say, 'God bless you,' as he pulled you off the ground," Rosenbach continued.

The pounding became too much for Rosenbach, and he left Phoenix after the '92 season. He played briefly in the Canadian Football League and tried to return to the NFL in 1995 with the New Orleans Saints. A ruptured disc in his back ended his time in the Big Easy, and Rosenbach transitioned to coaching. For the past two decades, he has served as a college assistant coach at various schools in the western United States. Currently, Rosenbach is an offensive assistant at the University of Montana.

MIKE PRICE

When asked in 2022 to reflect on his departure from Washington State after the 2002 season, Mike Price was candid. "Well, it was the hardest decision of my life, and probably the worst decision of my life to leave. So it is something I think about every day."

After spending time with his new Alabama Crimson Tide team in the spring of 2003, Price was at a golf tournament in Pensacola, Florida, in May of that year. *Sports Illustrated* would later report that, while at the tournament, Price visited a local strip club, and approximately $1,000 was charged to his hotel room by an unknown woman who was staying in Price's room. This incident was preceded by a reprimand from Alabama against Price for drinking in bars near the Tuscaloosa campus where students were present. By the end of the investigation into the strip club visit and room tab incident, Price was fired by Alabama before ever coaching a game. Coach Price vehemently denied the incidents and sued Time Warner/*Sports Illustrated* and settled the matter out of court. A year later, the University of Texas–El Paso hired him to be their new head coach. Price then turned a negative life experience into a positive when he led UTEP to two consecutive 8-4 seasons in 2004 and 2005 and bowl appearances after both seasons. The '04 season was a stunning turnaround for a program that had won six games total the previous three years, and Price was a finalist for Coach of the Year honors. In 2010, the Miners went to a third bowl game under Price after a 6-6 regular season. At the conclusion of the 2012 season, Price briefly retired from coaching. He returned to the Miners for the last seven games in 2017 when then–head coach Sean Kugler stepped down after five games. Price ended his time at UTEP with a 48-68 record and three bowl appearances. Currently, Price lives near Dennis Erickson in the Coeur d'Alene, Idaho area.

DREW BLEDSOE

In the second game of the 2001 NFL season, Bledsoe was running for his life from an onrushing New York Jets defense. As he reached the sideline, Jets linebacker Mo Lewis barrelled into him with a vicious hit. When he got up, Bledsoe didn't feel right. Team doctors escorted him to the training room and believed he had received a concussion. As it turned out, Lewis's hit had severed blood vessels in Bledsoe's chest, and the quarterback was bleeding internally. The injury caused him to miss the rest of the regular season, and his backup, second-year signal-caller Tom Brady, took his place. Little did anyone know that Brady would become one of the best quarterbacks in NFL history. Bledsoe came back for the '01 playoffs (after a Brady injury) to help win the AFC Championship game against the Pittsburgh Steelers. But Brady was named the starter for Super Bowl XXVII and helped the franchise win the game, 20–17 (the first of his seven Super Bowl victories).

The following year, Brady was named the Patriots' starter, and Bledsoe was traded to the Buffalo Bills, where he played through the 2004 season. In 2005, he signed with the Dallas Cowboys and was reunited with coach Bill Parcells. That season, he passed for over 3,000 yards for the ninth time in his career, which tied him for fourth in league history. Bledsoe would play with the Cowboys in 2006 and retire after the season. During his pro career, Bledsoe passed for 44,611 yards, 251 touchdowns and 206 interceptions. He was a four-time Pro Bowler, 1-1 in Super Bowls and the NFL's passing yards leader in 2004. Bledsoe currently resides with his family in Oregon. He also owns a successful winery in Walla Walla, Washington.

RYAN LEAF

After leaving the NFL, Leaf hit a rough patch in his life that played out in front of a national audience. In 2008, he was coaching quarterbacks at West Texas A&M when he was suspended after asking a player for a painkiller to help his ailing wrist. Leaf then resigned the following day. For the next several years, the former first-round pick was in the news for all the wrong reasons. In 2009, he was indicted for burglary and controlled substance charges in Texas. Three years later, he was arrested twice in his hometown of Great Falls, Montana, for burglary and drug charges. Months later, Leaf was sentenced to seven years in jail but was released after two years. By 2018, Leaf was working with Transcend Recovery Community to help patients dealing with addictions. He then found employment with ESPN in the summer of 2019 as a college football analyst. In 2020, Leaf was cited for misdemeanor domestic battery in California. PointsBet hired Leaf in the fall of 2022 to discuss college and NFL games and offer betting analysis.

JASON GESSER

After returning to WSU in 2014, Gesser worked in the school's athletic department for a few years, rising to the title of assistant director for the Cougar Athletic Fund by 2018. That same year, the university announced that several women had come forward accusing Gesser of sexual misconduct and harassment. WSU's student newspaper, the *Daily Evergreen*, published a story in September 2018 detailing its review of hundreds of pages of public records. Those records included harassment allegations against Gesser made by student interns, coworkers and even a nanny employed by the Gesser family. Some of the allegations dated back to 2014. The university conducted its own investigation, and the former quarterback was not involved. Gesser was not found guilty of any crime specifically, but he resigned from his position, and the school accepted his resignation.

"I am deeply saddened that recent circumstances in my private life have created a distraction for the department and university," Gesser wrote. "While I certainly never intended to hurt anyone, I believe it is best for all involved for me to move on. To the young woman that I made feel uncomfortable, I respectfully have a different recollection of the situation you've described," Gesser wrote, "but acknowledge that I should never have been in the situation in the first place, and I apologize. I truly never meant to cause you harm."

STEVE GLEASON

Lost in the feel-good story of Ryan Leaf and the Cougars' 1997 Rose Bowl season was sophomore linebacker Steve Gleason. Gleason was a native of Spokane, Washington, and was a Tasmanian Devil for the Gonzaga Prep High School Bullpups. By the time his senior season came to a close, Gleason was pursued by a number of Pac-10 schools, including Stanford University. However, according to Mike Price, the Cardinal made a mistake in underestimating Gleason. That error in judgment proved beneficial for WSU. "Stanford might have had a chance to get Steve, but their head coach told him he was too little to play at Stanford. So when Steve came to visit us next, he was pissed," recalled Price in 2022. "He was a leader, such a great kid and such a neat person."

After the '97 season, WSU won six combined games the next two years, which also happened to be Gleason's final two years with the program. Throughout those lean years, Gleason never gave up, and he continued to spur his teammates on, no matter the trial. In 2000, Gleason was not drafted by the NFL but was signed as an undrafted free agent by the Indianapolis Colts. The Colts cut him after the preseason, and Gleason was then signed by the New Orleans Saints. For the next several years, Gleason rarely cracked the Saints' starting lineup, but he was a notable special teams demon. Then, in August 2005, Hurricane Katrina crashed into southern Louisiana and devastated the New Orleans area. The Superdome (where the Saints played their home games) was used as a shelter of last resort for many of the area's residents. By the time the floodwaters from the storm dried, the structure of the stadium was badly damaged. That season, the Saints had to play all of their "home" games in other cities, and the end result was a 3-13 record.

In the face of such crippling adversity, the city of New Orleans pressed on and rebuilt itself. Instead of being demolished, the Superdome underwent a substantial remodeling before being declared structurally sound. In fact, the work on the stadium was finished in time for the 2006 NFL season. In Week 3, the Saints hosted their first home game in over a year on *Monday Night Football*. The Atlanta Falcons were in town and hoping to squash the Saints' emotional return home. Instead, the Superdome was rockin' with musical guests U2, and former president George H.W. Bush was part of the ceremonial coin toss. Remarkably, on just the fourth play of the game, Gleason became a permanent part of New Orleans Saints lore.

The Falcons were forced to punt, and Gleason lined up on the other side of the ball. As fate would have it, after the snap, a gaping hole in the middle of the line opened up, and Gleason snuck through. Just as Falcons punter Michael Koenen kicked the ball, Gleason came streaking in and blocked the punt. The ball bounced a few yards and was picked up by New Orleans cornerback Curtis Deloatch, who ran the ball into the end zone for a touchdown. Just like that, the Saints were on the scoreboard with 13:30 still remaining in the first quarter. Gleason was immediately mobbed by his teammates, and the Superdome was delirious with joy. There would be no letdown that evening for the emotionally charged Saints team. By the final whistle, they had made their triumphant return to the Big Easy with a resounding 23–3 victory and a 3-0 record. Years later, team management unveiled a statue of the play outside of the stadium, complete with Gleason's outstretched arms blocking the punt. The statue is simply titled *Rebirth*.

Gleason himself retired after the 2007 season and was diagnosed with ALS in 2011. As his body has slowly deteriorated from the disease, Gleason has refused to concede, as is his nature. Although he is now confined to a wheelchair and unable to speak, Gleason communicates through an electronic system that allows him to use his eyes to look at letters on a screen. Then, an automated voice speaks what Gleason has looked at through high-tech visual software. Recently, the Steve Gleason Institute for Neuroscience opened in Gleason's hometown of Spokane. The institute has partnered with Washington State University to help those suffering from ALS and its effects. In 2020, Gleason was recognized by Congress with the Congressional Gold Medal for his ALS work and his "no white flags" attitude. He is the first NFL player to receive the award.

REFERENCES

Prologue

Gordon Monson, "Monson: Dennis Erickson Is Almost 72. He Has Coached from Coast to Coast, Has Won National Titles, Was a Head Coach in the NFL—and He Is Pumped to Be Leading the Salt Lake Stallions," *Salt Lake Tribune*, February 9, 2019.

Chapter 1

Information regarding William Goodyear, William Dietz, "Babe" Hollingbery, WSU name changes, Mel Hein, Turk Edwards and Elmer Schwartz accessed via WSU library archives and footballfoundation.org.

Cougars name change: KREM.com, "Mascot Mania: How the Cougars Became the Cougars," July 2, 2020.

Jack Thompson quote: 247sports.com, "Destiny: How Legendary Jack Thompson Landed and Stayed at WSU," June 10, 2022.

Dennis Erickson quote: interview with author, February 2022.

Chapter 2

Dennis Erickson quote: Craig Smith, "Robert 'Pink' Erickson: 1924–2004; Father of NFL Coach Steeped in Game," *Seattle Times*, May 1, 2004.

Mike Price quotes: interview with author, February 2022.

Bart Wright, *Football Revolution: The Rise of the Spread Offense and How It Transformed College Football* (Lincoln: University of Nebraska Press, 2013).

Chapter 3

Wright, *Football Revolution*.

Dennis Erickson quote: interview with author, February 2022.

Chapter 4

Dennis Erickson and Mike Price quotes: interviews with author, February 2022.

Eric Yarber and Dennis Erickson information and quotes: Jerry Crowe, "Angry Wyoming Faces Ex-Coach: To His Former Team, Erickson Has Become a Rhinestone Cowboy," *Los Angeles Times*, September 12, 1987.

Cody Tucker, "My Cross to Bear," 7220sports.com, March 5, 2021.

Dennis Erickson Idaho and Wyoming information: interview with author, February 2022.

Tim Layden, *Blood, Sweat, and Chalk* (New York: Sports Illustrated Books, 2010).

Chapter 5

Chris Baker, "Quarterback in Waiting: Cardinals Rookie from Washington State Eager to Display His Talent in the NFL," *Los Angeles Times*, December 9, 1989.

Timm Rosenbach quotes: interview with author, March 2022.

WSU-UCLA game highlights and quotes from YouTube.

Rosenbach, Erickson and Cougars 1988 in-season quotes: archives of the *Spokesman-Review* (Spokane, WA).

247sports.com, "Cougs over No. 1 UCLA in 1988: Greatest WSU Victory of All Time?" October 29, 2013.

Chapter 6

"2022" quotes by Erickson, Price and Rosenbach: interviews with author, February and March 2022.

Baker, "Quarterback in Waiting."

NFL.com.

All other quotes obtained through the archives of the *Spokesman-Review*.

Chapter 7

Drew Bledsoe recruiting recollection and all other "2022" quotes by Mike Price: interview with author, February 2022.

Bledsoe, Price and Cougars 1992 in-season quotes: archives of the *Spokesman-Review*.

Bud Withers, "1992 Apple Cup Conjures Snowdust Memories," *Seattle Times*, November 19, 2002.

Chapter 8

Ryan Leaf, *596 Switch: The Improbable Journey From The Palouse to Pasadena* (Pullman, WA: Crimson Oak Publishing, 2011).

Leaf, Price and Cougars' 1997 in-season quotes: archives of the *Spokesman-Review*.

Nicholas J. Cotsonika, "'Mistake' Costs WSU Final Play," *Washington Post*, January 2, 1998.

Theo Lawson, "Members of WSU Cougars' 1997 Rose Bowl Team Return for 25-Year Reunion," *Seattle Times*, October 2, 2022.

Chapter 9

"2022" quotes by Mike Price: Interview with author, February and March 2022.

2002 in-season quotes were obtained through the archives of the *Spokesman-Review*.

Lewiston Tribune archives, December 29, 2002.

2012 Gesser quote: *Seattle Times*, November 21, 2012.

WSU: Cougars.com, November 23, 2002.
Seattlepi.com, November 17, 2003.

Chapter 10

Leach hired by WSU: *Spokesman-Review*, November 30, 2011.
"2022" quotes by Mike Leach: interview with author, May 2022.
Remaining quotes from chapter: archives of the *Spokesman-Review*.

Epilogue

Timm Rosenbach "2022" quotes: interview with author, February 2022.
Ira Berkow, "Walking Away While He Still Can; Troubled and Fearing Injury, Timm Rosenbach Quit Football," *New York Times*, October 3, 1993.
Mike Price "2022" quote: interview with author, February 2022.
Don Yaeger, "How He Met His Destiny at a Strip Club Mike Price: Fired," *Sports Illustrated*, May 12, 2003.
Jason Gesser: *Star Advertiser* (Honolulu, HI), September 18, 2018.
Steve Gleason "2022" Mike Price quote: interview with author, February 2022.

ABOUT THE AUTHOR

Ben Donahue has worked for over twenty-five years in sports at the K–12, college and professional levels. His experience includes athletic director, game-day operations and guest relations, football operations, coach and baseball scout. Currently, he is a contributing writer for brownsnation. com and profootballhistory.com. This is his first book.

Visit us at
www.historypress.com